Miraclefesting:

Inspiring Stories To Help You Recognize and Create Everyday Miracles In Your Life

By Jennifer Blanchard
Vanessa LeVan
Dana Rivera

Table of Contents

Welcome to Miraclefesting xi

Step 1: ASK 1

  Vanessa's Stories

    Introduction: Vanessa LeVan 3

    And There He Was.... 5
      Lesson: Know what you want; no gray area, stand firm

    The Heart Always Knows 9
      Lesson: Be honest, be brave, be clear

    Blush—Still Going Strong 12 Years Later 18
      Lesson: Listen to your heart and take inspired action

    Ms. Fancy Pants 21
      Lesson: Be clear on what you want; again, no gray area

    I Manifested Lisa Nichols (and She Doesn't Even Know About It) 26
      Lesson: Know exactly what you want and be willing to ask for it

    And Then There Was Tony Robbins 32
      *Lesson: I was clear I would see Tony Robbins...and I was
      open to where that might lead*

And Boom, There It Is   36

Lesson: Sometimes you don't even have to ask when you're open to receiving

Your Wish Is My Command   38

Lesson: Stop and notice the small things; there are miracles within

It Could Have Been Me On The Wheatie's Box   40

Lesson: Clarity when asking is key

And There She Was, Right Down the Street   43

Lesson: Being clear on what you NEED, presents opportunities

In Conclusion   46

Step 2: BELIEVE   48

Jennifer's Stories

Introduction: Jennifer Blanchard   51

How I Manifested the Dog of My Dreams   55

Lesson: Sometimes you have to hold out

How I Get Front-Row Parking Spots Everywhere I Go   59

Lesson: Make what you want your "new normal" and it will be

How I Manifested $2,500 Cash in 3 Hours   62

Lesson: You can have any-freaking-thing you set your mind to and take action on

How I Manifested A Free Car   65

Lesson: Know what you want; believe you can have it; trust that it's already done the moment you ask for it

The Aerator Email   68

Lesson: The things you want can show up fast when you're not attached to when, how or where you get them

How I Manifested A Spot In A Sold-Out 9:30 A.M. SoulCycle Class   70

Lesson: Make the decision and wear blinders to all other possibilities

How I Manifested Money to Buy the Perfect Blue Dress   74

Lesson: You must stand your ground on what you are now deciding is true for you

The Night I Almost Got Hit By A Car   80

Lesson: Trust the nudges you receive

How I Became A Bestselling Author On Amazon   83

Lesson: Commit to acting on all Divine Downloads, soul nudges, and inspired ideas

How I Quit My Day Job to Take My Writing Business Full-Time   90

Lesson: Make the leap and the Universe will support you

In Conclusion   95

Step 3: RECEIVE   97

Dana's Stories

Introduction: Dana Rivera   99

The Miracle About the Wallet   102

Lesson: Decide what you want and follow your inner guidance to get it

The Grapefruit Spoon Miracle   105

Lesson: Ask and stay open to the possibilities

The Chapstick Miracle   108

Lesson: Practice receiving without judging the source

The Miracle Message   110

Lesson: Ask from a place of love, not fear

My Painting Miracle 114

Lesson: Love things into your life

The India Trip 117

Lesson: Keep your desires alive and stay open to receiving them

Mulch Can Be Miraculous Too 120

Lesson: We are angels for each other

The Surprise Income Miracle 122

Lesson: We don't need to know the 'how'

Housekeeper at the Door 124

Lesson: We attract what we think about with love and curiosity

Car Accident Angels 126

Lesson: Angels are always with us

Muscle Testing Angel 129

Lesson: Our growth and expansion are always supported

Island-Hopping 130

Lesson: Love it into your reality

Hurricanes Need Love Too 134

Lesson: Our focused love is more powerful than we realize

My Clothing Business Blessing 136

Lesson: Follow your desires AND your gut

The Man and the Dog 140

Lesson: There are no coincidences

A Miracle Since Writing This Book 147

Lesson: You attract what you energetically broadcast

In Conclusion 152

About the Authors 154

More From the Authors 157

About the Cover Artist 159

Welcome to Miraclefesting

You may have watched *The Secret*, or read a new-age spirituality book, and heard the process for manifesting what you desire described as:

1. **Ask**
2. **Believe**
3. **Receive**

This is pretty general manifestation advice. And while it's not wrong, it's also not detailed enough to be super helpful.

That's why we wrote this book—to inspire you with our stories of manifesting everyday miracles in our lives, and to give you the specific, detailed steps we took within each of those three general manifestation steps, so you can do the same in your life.

While all of our stories have each of the three steps of the manifestation process in them, our personal manifestation styles focus in on one of the steps over the others. So that's how we've divided the book up.

We hope you enjoy Miraclefesting, and that it inspires you to create everyday miracles in your life too.

~ **Jennifer, Vanessa and Dana**

"You've literally been performing miracles your entire life."
—**Notes From the Universe, by Mike Dooley**

Step 1: ASK

Vanessa's Stories

Introduction: Vanessa LeVan

This book has been a lesson for me. I'm always looking for opportunities to learn, but I had not imagined I'd learn so much on the subject of the book I already thought I knew well enough to write about!

Miraclefesting; Manifesting; Making Things Happen; call it what you will. Here is a short little book that I hope inspires you, intrigues you and kicks you in the butt to expect, ask for and receive more out of life. In your hands is 100-plus years of cumulative knowledge the three of us have compiled on how we've gotten what we've wanted in life. Even as one of the contributing authors having a hand in writing this, I've been so inspired by Jen's and Dana's stories that I got right to work on bringing some more awesomeness into my life.

Not until we all submitted our portions of the book did we realize that we each came at this business of Miraclefesting very differently; each with our own beliefs on what works for us. But now, the possibilities really do seem endless. It's powerful knowing that we have three ways that work beautifully together to implement getting what we want effortlessly. You will learn all three of our clear, concise strategies so you, too, can have everything you dream of.

If only I had learned this earlier!! Imagine now what I can make happen!

This new implementable knowledge has filled me with an excitement and calmness knowing that I can have the marriage of my dreams, bring my company to the level I desire, and travel to the destinations I can't wait to explore.

I hope that you are as inspired by this book as I have been, and are ready to implement and hone your own skills in getting what you want.

~ **Vanessa**

And There He Was....

Lesson: Know what you want; no gray area, stand firm

I am a really good manifester. There I said it; right at the beginning. Let's just get it out there; I'm a manifester. But truth be told, I cringe at that word. It seems so woo-woo and I like to think I'm practical.

It's so "spiritual" and I'm a lifelong Catholic. It's so airy-fairy and I'm grounded. It's weird, but I think I'm normal (just don't ask my brother). It's not professional and strategic, and I'm a woman running a successful business.

But like it or not, even though I'm not the moon-and-stone-worshiping, energy-healing, mantra-saying goddess, I'm still a great manifester (aka Miraclefester). After all, these are everyday miracles we're talking about, that really are the meaning of life.

I know who I am, what I want, and stand firm in my values. No guessing involved. I'm a mom to two and a wife to my high school love. I'm a boutique owner and love building a business.

I'm happiest listening to waves lapping and the smell of the beach or the smell of the sun warming up pine needles underneath the towering Ponderosa's. I love flowers in my yard, watching the blooms unfurl to see what beauty will be revealed that day. I love the sun (ideally at 75 degrees) and believe it heals the heart and soul. And beautiful fabrics, they speak to me, begging me to create something from their yardage. That's a glimpse of my black and white soul.

I strive to make each day valuable, productive and peaceful in my heart.

I'm over here conquering real struggles using the power of "getting out of God's way" and good old-fashioned "pull myself up by my bootstraps" for what's been thrown my way. So with that, I'm going to refer to myself, not as a manifester, but a Make Things Happen Girl! Sounds so much more....normal. With my newly defined "Make Things Happen Girl" persona, I'll own it; I'm really good at getting what I want and always have been.

My husband was one of my earliest and obviously most profound miracles, as he's now been hanging around more than half my life. At age sixteen, I saw this good-looking, skinny, Wrangler-wearing senior cowboy walking past the health building with his friends. Unbeknownst to him, my sites were set. He was a goner. I'd just set eyes on my husband.

I could tell you what he was wearing; how they were walking in a line, shoulder-to-shoulder, and how our eyes met. Poor guy never stood a chance against my "powers." Try as he might to run away several times throughout the years, I lassoed that one and never let him go.

What can I say? Love.

Have the last 27 years been blissfully idyllic? Are anyone's? Absolutely not. We were children when we met; growing, discovering and developing into different versions of ourselves. But I know I'm there for him, he's there for me. We are each other's person. I know I push him to step into his best self and he pushes me to be more understanding and nice. We are the definition of balance with one moment the scale tipping to the left then to the right, but always coming back to center. Besides, we still sleep touching each and every night and my heart still skips a beat when I hear his truck pull up each night and he walks through the door.

I guess it really is love.

I'm sure you're a great Make Things Happen Girl or Guy too. We all are, but are we using this power to its greatest potential? If we shuffle through the files and thumb through the Rolodexes of our lives up to this point, I'm sure we can all come up with a list of people, boyfriends, husbands, trips, things, money, no money, and all other manner of junk/treasures/experiences we've brought into our lives.

And let's be honest with ourselves here, because sometimes we may not want to believe we got exactly what we asked for when we look back and can see it wasn't necessarily the best thing for us. Hindsight's 20/20.

Whether we like it or not, for the most part, our life is a culmination of what we ask for, or conversely, don't ask for, and our willingness to **listen wholeheartedly and act upon the words of our soul**. Words, whispers, nudges or signs; however your intuition speaks to you.

The Heart Always Knows
Lesson: Be honest, be brave, be clear

I have found that each of us seems to be good at manifesting in certain areas of our life. Maybe for you, it's money, physical goods, experiences, business deals or clients. For me, I'm best at manifesting people in my life. I have quite a few stories of bringing those into my life that have given me experiences and teachings when I needed them most. They've brought nuggets of information and inspiration and lessons that have had lasting ripple effects that continue to this day.

When there's something I need to learn, whether I know it or not—BAM!—I have a new person in my life to teach it to me.

Have you ever had those distinct moments in time where everything falls into place and then the cherry is placed on top, as if by the hands of God himself? Which it probably was God himself, unless you have the gifts of Samantha from Bewitched (yes, I'm dating myself), and all you have to do is wiggle your nose, and

POOF! There's your greatest moment's desire. A time when your thoughts became your reality without much, if any, effort at all.

Now if only we can learn to do this on demand with the consistency of drinking water. Can you imagine how rich we'd be in life? The people and experiences; the trips we'd take and the beautiful things we'd be surrounding ourselves with!

But interestingly enough, as I sit here and write this, I find myself shrinking and this thought pops into my head: *"Oh, that would be too often to get what I want."* Say what?! That thought, right there, my friends, is what prevents an overflow of goodness and abundance in my life, and if your thoughts follow in the footsteps of mine, your abundance too! I'm allowing myself only trickles. But why?

My inner critic and saboteur are always hard at work filling me with doubt. Here are some of my most prevalent thoughts: *"I don't need that," "I'll suffer through this;" "things aren't always easy for you," "marriage is hard," "you have a house, why should it be nicer?" "your windows are broken and that's a metaphor for your life"* (this is actually a story I tell myself). It's crazy that I have within my power, the ability to create what I want, and yet these ridiculous thoughts run my life and often not for the better. It's all backed up by these elaborate stories I tell; convincing myself this is why things are the way they are.

I've created this life and some of it I don't even like! This makes me realize I HAVE GOT TO STOP WITH THE STORIES.

Here is what I know for a fact, as a Make Things Happen Girl. When I have a thought, a want, or a need, and zero attachments to how it will happen with zero beliefs about it, and it's backed with 100% certainty (more on this later), it easily comes into my life, without much or any effort.

Why, oh why, then, do I make things harder than they need to be? Why do I cling to stories that make my life harder? I'm realizing life doesn't have to be a struggle; only if I want it to be. The problem is that sometimes the known is safer than the unknown, although the unknown is often better! We cling to the past and as Sandra Yancey, the founder of eWomen famously says, *"When the past comes calling, hang up on it. It has nothing new for you."* Isn't that brilliant?

Now back to those moments where your dream shows up. I have at least a few distinct episodes that seem frozen in time, where I can think, *"Whoa! that showed up after I said I wanted it. How did I make that happen? I surely didn't take active pursuit of it. It didn't take hard work, nor did it take wrestling the dragons to their death to get it...it just happened."* Not that I can't get results through hard work, beating my head against the wall and inflicting pain; because obviously everyone can, but in the long run, how did those "opportunities" work out?

I can tell you, not very well for me. Every-single-darn-time I've had to work really hard at something that didn't come easy and I dreaded some part of it or didn't follow my intuition, it has not turned out well. Lesson learned. I've now accepted that if something is hard and I'm trying to convince myself that I like it or rationalize even a piece of it, I'm really just trying to convince myself of something I already know in my heart.

The heart always knows. Listen. Be honest with yourself. Don't be afraid to move on.

Keep in mind that there are actually people who thrive on what you are resisting. It's meant for them, not you, no matter how great the opportunity. I'm certainly not saying don't stretch yourself and try new things, because that is also very important. But you know when you know and you also know when you're just making excuses. It's time to be really honest with yourself. This isn't always easy, be brave. Remember, there are those that truly like to master cleaning someone else's teeth, or dig holes in the hard ground, or build computers, but that doesn't mean you do. Shockingly, there are people that like to cold-call a business and offer them the greatest new credit card service. I gave it a try, stepped out of my comfort zone. Not for me! And there is someone for everyone, your prince charming is waiting. If your dreamboat is a man with a low, stringy ponytail wearing sandals, just come to Denver, he's here.

Stick by your values, because you already know. We know within seconds if this opportunity/job/person is right. If something really is right for you, it's going to be an "*I LOVE IT!*" Or, "*I LOVE HIM!*" Or, "*I LOVE this thing*," whatever it is. Your heart knows. But are you listening?

It's become clear to me that you don't have to chant mantras and affirmations. You don't have to future-cast (pretending you already have it). You don't have to put it on your vision board. You don't have to worship and pray and beg for it and you don't even have to believe you're going to get it. All you have to do is know with 100% clarity and certainty that you want it.

Not one moment of wishy-washy-ness either. No questions, no parameters, no rules on how it will arrive in your life. Maybe when these restrictions do arise alongside of our want, it may mean we aren't really ready for it and that's why some resistance is accompanying it. Most likely there's a lesson in the struggle(s) we'll encounter as we work towards that thing we say we want. Or maybe it's our inner saboteur hard at work. I haven't figured that part out yet, but what I have figured out is the formula for getting what you want.

Know what you want without a doubt. Ask for it with clarity and then Get Out Of God's Way. Period.

I've been pretty good in the clarity piece and sitting back and watching piece of this formula for a long time, but putting the thought and words to "get-out-of-God's-way" was only introduced to me this past year by my friend Shawn, and wow, it's been powerful.

My vision board makes this very clear. The 'have gots' and the 'haven't gots.' I can now see my 'haven't gots' all have attachments to them. Most are things I want for my house and yard that have been on there for at least two years and haven't happened yet. A gorgeous fire pit sitting on a stone patio surrounded by different size boulders. A beautiful stone fireplace with natural, reclaimed wood beams. A natural stone shower in a herringbone pattern and a heavy white linen shower curtain. I know from the depths of my soul I've got the shower curtain part taken care of, but the rest, not so much. Or so I've been thinking.

My husband is a contractor and I have been very actively and consciously expecting him to spearhead these projects and get them done. These are in his wheelhouse, not mine. But…these are on my vision board, not his. The fire pit isn't his dream; it's mine. He doesn't care that we have moldy tile in the shower; I do.

I've put so many attachments on how these things are supposed to happen and get done, and they all revolve around him. I've literally been trying to force them into happening. Duh. Of course they haven't happened; there are all kinds of parameters attached to them. I might as well take the pictures off of my vision board until I can release all of that, otherwise having them on there is pointless.

I can easily see the things that do magically happen from my vision board are things I definitely want, maybe even need, but they're more of a pipedream. Great and exciting if it happens, but if it doesn't, oh well. No timelines attached to them, and no sadness if it doesn't happen. Also no stress in wondering how they will happen, nor thinking it's someone's responsibility to make them happen. Just pictures of things I want and possibly need to make my life richer on the soul level.

This year I had Mexico on my board and I went twice! My cousin invited us to his destination wedding and then our neighbors randomly asked if we wanted to go because they'd be kid-free for a week. *Sure! Why not?*

I had South Carolina on my board for two years and guess what? I'm going in November 2018 because my son joined the Army and is at Bootcamp in, guess where? South Carolina. We'll be going to his graduation ceremony.

Could I have forced that one to happen? I don't think the Army would've taken my request seriously if I asked for Chase to be sent to Fort Jackson, as if I even knew there was a base in South Carolina! These were pipe-dreams that I'd be excited about if they happened, but not sad if they didn't. But was I sure I wanted them? Yes, 100% sure.

Now, down the road, I may have taken action to plan vacations there and make these happen, as I have Mexico in the past, but for now, they were just places I knew with certainty I wanted to go but had no timelines or parameters around them.

See the difference?

Side Note: I think it's important to have a board that is next to your vision board where you move everything to once it does happen. You want to be able to see visually what you've brought into your life and then a pattern becomes clear for you on how you got it.

I've had an interesting thought about vision boarding or dreaming about what you want. I was chatting with a friend and she voiced something that I had recently just considered as well. Do we cut out pictures, quotes, and words and plaster them all over a board because that's what we want to bring into our lives? Or do we put it on our board because it's already in our future but just now coming into our consciousness? Classic egg-before-the-chicken type of question! Just something to ponder over coffee in the morning.

To sum up what has helped me become a Make Things Happen Girl; I stand firm in what I want. If I waver at all, I know that means I don't want it on some level. Period. That can be a hard pill to swallow. There may be reasons I don't want it, subconsciously, like believing it's not the time or it's not meant to be. But whatever the reason, I don't actually want it if a *"but…"* pops in. Oh, I can rationalize it until the cows come home that I do desire it, but the quicker I can be honest with myself that, on some level, I'm not ready for it, the sooner I can get ready for it. All of those *"but…"* thoughts are putting restrictions and parameters on "it" and how God can make it happen. It's now dead in the water.

How great and freeing would it be if the second a *"but…"* comes into the picture I can take the want off the list or vision board and just accept and be totally okay that it's not in the cards right now and let it go? Imagine how free we'd be from the burdens and shoulds of trying to work towards something that's never going to happen in the current conditions anyways!

This is where resistance comes from. It's the excuses and stories I want more than what I say I want. I may be able to wrangle it into happening, through hard work; blood, sweat, and tears, but it won't be effortless and fun and maybe even against my better judgment, as discussed previously.

You know those things I'm talking about! Usually, in the aftermath, we can look back and see whatever it was we wanted, that we tried to force or didn't have any fun doing, proves to have been a wrong move. When I've pushed forward with something that takes convincing on a daily basis, I can chalk it up to there being a lesson or experience I really wanted/needed to learn and that's why I subconsciously refused to take the easy route. A lesson I didn't know I needed but was made the wiser for it.

When I listen to my inner knowing and am 100% clear either way, yes or no; the right decision has been made. This is being true to myself and it works out each and every time.

Richard Branson is the perfect example. Now I don't know him personally—shocking I know—but he appears to always have that big grin on his face and is enjoying every single moment. His light and clarity shine through, even in a photo! He is clearly following the fun!

> *"My general attitude to life is to enjoy every minute of every day. I never do anything with a feeling of, 'Oh God, I've got to do this today.'"*
> **—Richard Branson**

Blush—
Still Going Strong 12 Years Later
Lesson: Listen to your heart and take inspired action

Dana (one of the co-authors of this book) and I built a clothing business based on the "Richard Branson" principle—Fun. From the very start our motto was, *"If it's not fun, we're not doing it."*

We met when our daughters were in kindergarten and our first "date" was sewing pillows together. A girl after my own heart! I think we talked more than we sewed because I don't remember any pillows coming out of that. Several years later, we were both stay-at-home moms and the kids were getting older. We had become better friends and were looking for something to do. We were presented with an opportunity to sell a seasonal clothing line. We quickly realized we wanted the freedom to choose our own lines and styles and we wanted to carry the inventory and form our own company. *Blush* Was Born!

We went home and booked tickets to L.A. right away. We called Dana's cousin (who was working in a showroom) for valuable insight and a place to stay and we got to work planning our first trunk show. We had 100% clarity on starting our own clothing business; no wavering and no doubts.

Twelve years later, turns out we were right! I'm now running *Blush Out West* with my daughter, Wren, and Dana is on a break from clothing and working on *Fabulous Bubbles*. I'm still having fun and wouldn't want to be doing anything else! There have been a couple of times over those 12 years that I chased after another business opportunity because of money or needing change, but it never worked out, and I always returned to the world of schlepping clothes.

When something is easy, fun, and brings joy I know I'm on the right path.

Several years before Dana and I started *Blush*, I had looked into opening a children's clothing boutique in downtown Napa, California. In Napa at that time, one landlord held most of the downtown real estate hostage. I remember standing outside of one of his storefronts with him and he literally told me, "*No, I won't rent to you; your business will fail.*"

I was put out at the time, and thought, "*How dare he tell me I'll fail!*" But luckily I listened because he was probably right. Downtown Napa was NOT happening at the time; I had two very small kids and no clue what to do.

Many years later, after moving to Colorado, I was a co-owner of a couple of storefront boutiques along with two other ladies, and I can say with certainty, I would've been in way over my head had I moved forward with the children's store many moons before that.

But the timing was perfect when Dana and I jumped in head first with *Blush* and we knew it!

Ms. Fancy Pants

Lesson: Be clear on what you want; again, no gray area

I know one of the teachings of manifesting is to do affirmations so you embed in your brain a new belief. I call bull on this one. In my experience, I don't even have to believe I'll get what I'm asking for.

In fact, one of the biggest things I've miraclefested was something I was actually embarrassed to want, and not in a million years did I think I'd get it. Yes, I was 100% sure I wanted it, but definitely didn't think I'd be getting it.

Here's the story of the biggest and fanciest thing I've made happen: a vehicle. A vehicle I didn't think I deserved. A fancy car that I wouldn't even drive for three weeks because I was embarrassed by its luxury.

It's even more hilarious that I had set my eyes on a vehicle because I'm not even a car person. I really don't like things with motors. A big negative to motorcycles, ATVs or jet skis for me. They're loud, ugly and dangerous. Give me a set of skis or my own two feet or even a horse and I'm happy to tag along. Ask me to ride one of those with a motor; no thanks!

My son once asked me, "*But mom, don't you want to KNOW how your car engine works?*"

"*No Chase, I don't. I really don't.*"

It used to be my dream to be Laura Ingalls Wilder. I spent hours making griddle cakes and running around in prairie skirts. No Joke. I would prefer a horse and buggy, but alas, I'm not Amish, so it's really not a practical solution for me.

So, yes, I love having a reliable vehicle that is clean, well-maintained and safe, with good, aggressive tires. I'm a wimp in the snow. But when I saw this model of vehicle—that I ended up miraclefesting— driving down the road, I *realllly* liked it. That even shocked me!

The world had recently been introduced to luxury SUVs; an SUV that set the standard for years to come. There I was, contentedly driving my Ford Explorer through town, with my two young kids in the back when THE one and only Pearl-White Escalade in Napa drove by me.

My eyes followed it and the pretty woman driving it; I can still picture her. Shortly thereafter the thought popped into my mind, "*I want one of those.*"

Up until that point, I'd never seen a car that I actually wanted. The couple of vehicles I had previously purchased were practical, nice and served their purpose. A nice little Sentra to get me to and from college; and once that first baby came I quickly realized we needed four doors, so the Explorer was perfect. But I wanted this Escalade like I'd never wanted any other thing with a motor, even to this day. So Silly!! But it was a beauty and I do love beautiful things; just usually in the form of pretty houses, nature, the beach, fabrics and of course tufted furniture.

A few days later, I was chatting with my cousin and I casually mentioned that I was going to get an Escalade. Here's why I say I don't think you have to believe with every fiber of your being that you'll be getting what you say you want. When I got off the phone with her, I was actually embarrassed that I had said I was getting an Escalade. I berated myself for saying something so foolish, as if we could afford one, and who did I think I was wanting one of the most expensive, fancy cars on the road?

As if! But the key was, I wanted it; I was very clear on that. And since I didn't believe for one second I'd be getting one, there were zero attachments or conditions or bargaining on how I was going to get this car.

Fast-forward a few weeks. My husband comes home from work on a Friday afternoon and tells me to come outside. Parked in front of our house on the street is, not his truck, but a Pearl-White Escalade.

"*Do you want this?*" he asked.

Keep in mind I hadn't even told him I wanted one of these! This happened when new construction was booming, and there was a landscaping company on his job site that was doing so well they were buying new vehicles every few months. They asked my husband if he'd want to buy it for his wife, and they said, "*take it home to your wife for the weekend and see if she likes it.*"

It had 14,000 miles on it. And I liked it. So we bought it and then it sat in the driveway for three weeks because I was too embarrassed to drive it. I just kept loading the kids into the Explorer until it sold, and then I had no choice but to move the car seat, booster, and kids into my new luxurious ride.

This car practically became a family member. We had it for fourteen years and it kept us safe. It was the most reliable car ever and handled beautifully in the snow after we moved to Colorado and it was big enough to house us for some time if we ever became homeless; we'd each almost have our own row to make our own. It hauled my kids from elementary school to high school, carted hay and grain, baseball equipment, snowboards, airsoft guns and loads of kids. It was perfect for a girls night out because ALL the girls could fit and of course, it carried loads and loads of clothes for my boutique business.

When I eventually downsized into a new car I bought another Cadillac, of course. It had treated us so well! Then the Escalade became my daughter's first car and got her to and from college, safe and sound. When we sold it, with over 200,000 miles, I actually cried! That car had protected my family and was a constant, strong presence through some years when nothing else was.

So, yes, I miraclefested a car, but not just any old car!

I Manifested Lisa Nichols
(And She Doesn't Even Know About It)
Lesson: Know exactly what you want and be willing to
ask for it

The Escalade was a big, expensive, physical thing that showed up out of nowhere, but what I'm mostly really good at is Making People Happen; bringing them into my life. I manifested Author and Speaker, Lisa Nichols, and she doesn't even know it!

If you don't know who she is, look her up; you'll be glad you did. She's a transformational coach, speaker, and author, and every word that comes out of her mouth is gold. I had been a groupie following her for quite some time; hanging on her words in every video and Facebook Live I could find. Soaking in each magical word she released.

The woman is a life changer and I was obsessed. In a good way. Dana was fortunate to be a part of a small mastermind that had a group call scheduled with Lisa Nichols and she was able to give me the recording to listen to. I was in heaven!

At the time, for a brief transitional period, I had taken a break from the boutique and I fancied myself a guide to help women bring more joy into their lives through a twelve-week program I had written with my good friend, Karen. They say you teach what you most need to learn and I was in a deep-dive phase of figuring out who I was now that my kids were older and I'd been married for a long time.

I certainly wasn't the carefree newlywed who got pregnant on the beaches of Tahiti (OK, bungalow), or the mom taxi, carting kids anymore, or a traditional career woman who at least knew who she was at work. I was someone, but I needed to redis-cover who that someone was. The content of our twelve-week program, workshops, and retreats was really good and for about a year we were able to touch quite a few women's lives so deeply and profoundly that one of the women recently revealed we had literally saved her life.

So even though it was a blip in time for me and not something I felt inclined to continue long-term, it was exactly what I needed, along with the handful of women we were able to guide through to the next phase of their lives.

We got out of God's way; listened to our intuition and had fun. We were 100% sure it was what we should be doing at that moment in time. That's powerful. Thanks to my husband Shawn and Karen's husband, we were supported through offer-ing these programs in this pivotal year of growth and guiding other women and ourselves to become who we are today.

Back to Lisa; it ties in, I promise.

During this year of running these women's programs, we set a really big goal of sponsoring and producing a large event for hundreds of women. An outdoor event, with lots of activities and bustling with energy. Kind of like the atmosphere of a 5k or 10k race, but without the race.

We were in the beginning planning stages and my dream was to have Lisa Nichols as the keynote speaker. If I could only talk to her, how could she say no to an event with hundreds of women coming together as a community to bond, grow, and create? Or something like that. But how was I going to talk to Lisa Nichols? Did she have an agent? Would I ever get through? Should I write her?

Lisa was getting closer to my world every day, as evidenced by the recorded coaching call Dana sent my way. I just had no idea how close. God works in mysterious ways!

If only we could physically see the filaments weaving together behind the scenes. Connecting the dots, detouring this way and that to bring people, places, and things into our realities, we'd be astounded, I'm sure! I picture them to be like a switch-board; little bulbs lighting up as each of our clear "wants" makes its way to us, ping-ponging through the world. Most of which we don't see or know about.

I picture my Blush Pink light bulb flashing as filaments are busy at work connecting. This visual really drives home the point that we need to keep our eye on the prize and not get distracted by all of the junk and negativity that creeps in, so that our true desires can ping-pong their way to us.

Karen and I had also been hitting the networking trail, and getting out and meeting lots of new people, and making connections. A few weeks later (this seems to be my manifesting timeline), we were virtually introduced to a woman through Facebook Messenger who we set up a time to chat with over coffee. We had similar missions of helping and bringing together women. We met her at a Starbucks right down the road from my house and shared what each of us was working on. At one point I was sharing our vision for this big event and that my dream was to have Lisa Nichols as our Keynote speaker. I mentioned how inspiring she is and that I was slightly obsessed with her. The woman replied with, "*What if I told you that you could meet her? Nobody knows about this yet, but my friend is bringing her to Denver for an intimate event they're putting on and she needs volunteers to help out.*"

YES! Of Course! Sign me up.

We actually did know the gal who was putting on the event, but unbeknownst to me, she had been privately coaching with Lisa Nichols for a couple of years. They had become quite close and were co-hosting this event.

You never know what is brewing behind the scenes. Pink light bulb flashing.

Fast forward to the day of the event. There were about sixty to seventy women in attendance, and Lisa Nichols was everything I had dreamed. All that and a bag of chips! She is a mighty powerhouse with words of wisdom and applicable tips and tricks to hack your brain. She really makes you think about and realize where you may be holding yourself back.

At the end of the event, she hosted a very intimate session for those who wanted to continue to hang out, where shoes got kicked off, she grabbed a quick meal and glass of wine and answered any questions anyone had.

This is where she also does her big sell and even if you aren't going to be investing in yourself at that level, it is still worth hanging out for those extra couple of hours and soaking in every last minute with her.

Also offered by Lisa Nichols and her co-host that day was an online six-month coaching program that was very affordable where we'd be meeting on Zoom (video conferencing) monthly. I happily signed up for this program and was astonished that on these Zoom calls where Lisa actually called on us by name, at most, fifteen ladies would show up live. I wouldn't have missed one for the world. Sometimes only six of us would be there!

This program didn't get started for several months after the event, and by this time, the grand women's event that Karen and I had been envisioning, wasn't going to happen. We were no longer interested in hosting and planning something like this. I had realized there were amazing transformational women's events everywhere and it wasn't my responsibility to put one on. I could just attend and not have the headache. It was a season that had passed for me and I was really focusing on my clothing business again. But it did not go unnoticed by me that had we still wanted to do the event, I was in a situation where I literally could have asked Lisa Nichols, over Zoom, face-to-face, if she'd be our keynote speaker.

Not that she would've said yes, or maybe she would have, but the opportunity was placed in front of me on a silver platter. And I worried over how in the heck I would get in contact with her all those months before.

Wow. I just needed to trust!

The idea had seemed so big, I had no idea where to even start. Even as I write this, I'm seeing how those filaments are swirling around in the backgrounds of our lives, bringing things, people, and places together; getting shorter and shorter, lighting up with the magic of connections.

All you have to do is know what you want; trust and get out of God's way. I could never have even dreamed up this situation on my own.

And Then There Was Tony Robbins

Lesson: I was clear I would see Tony Robbins...and I was open to where that might lead

One of my big dreams this last year was to go to a Tony Robbins conference. I believe it was Dana who introduced him to me too. Where would I be if I'd never met Dana?!

Of course the conferences he's known for and I've heard about are his big multi-day venues, so that is what I had envisioned myself going to when I said I'd be going to see Tony Robbins this year. I'd looked up dates and actually, the cousin's Mexico wedding I mentioned earlier, fell on the same dates as the conference that was closest to us, and my husband said he'd rather go to Mexico.

So Mexico it was. Tony Robbins would have to be at a later date. Or so I thought.

Sometime in late winter/early spring, my friend Shawn—not husband Shawn—asked if I wanted to go see Tony Robbins since she knew I was a fan. Well, yes, I did want to go see Tony Robbins and it just so happened he was coming to Denver.

I knew nothing about the event. I just happily said yes and Shawn got our tickets. It was a no-brainer. And wow, was it ever.

There were so many filaments weaving its way around and I believe still at work six months later; where do I even start!?

First of all, we got there early so had seats right on the ground level where Tony walks around and high fives people. We didn't get a high five but probably could've had we really wanted to. We were very close to him, as this was a fairly small crowd, compared to the thousands I've seen packed into his other events.

Secondly, Tony really talks a lot about going after what you want and what's holding you back and why we don't move forward. This was really driven home to my heart because that ground floor where we were sitting was actually the dirt arena (covered, of course) for the Denver Stock Show Arena. This was ironic to me because a couple of years prior, my brother and sister-in-law had taken home one of the biggest prizes granted in their industry on that very arena floor I was sitting on.

They had bred and raised the Grand Champion Prospect Steer, which is a HUGE accomplishment in the cattle world. I know this probably doesn't mean much to most reading this book, but this is right up there with winning the Super Bowl or at least making it to the game.

My brother had been working on the genetics of his herd for twenty-plus years and had finally hit the jackpot. His dream is to run his cattle herd full-time and not have a stressful sales job in addition to that, where he has to meet quotas, drive hundreds of miles a day, deal with client accounts, etc. He won't quit his job because he's not a risk taker, he's comfortable and he's afraid. Afraid of taking the leap; having less security. Afraid of trusting himself even though he just proved he is a force in the industry.

It made me sad for him as I listened to Tony Robbins deliver this very message. Now don't get me wrong, he is living a great life; has a healthy family, beautiful ranch, and is obviously able to accomplish big things with his "side gig," but his true dream is withering on the vine. I think others believe in him more than he believes in himself and that's the part that makes me sad.

Last of all, on this powerful day, there was an offer that was presented to attend another event, free of charge, which I signed up for. At that event, months later, I met a guy who was an integral part of my son's decision to join the Army. He was a Green Beret who had recently retired from the Army and was so gracious to meet with Chase, me and my husband on multiple occasions throughout this past summer. He answered hours of questions, gave lots of insight, and talked to us about the experiences available to Chase if he were to move forward in enlisting. He even took Chase to the shooting range and gave him lots of tips.

If I hadn't gone to Tony Robbins and signed up for and gone to this other event months later and then been placed in a random eight-person group with this Green Beret, Chase may still be sitting in his room playing video games trying to figure out what he wants to be when he grows up! But as of today, he'll be graduating from boot camp in two weeks!

Pink light bulbs going off.

And Boom, There It Is

Lesson: Sometimes you don't even have to ask when you're open to receiving

As I sit here, in a local coffee shop, writing the above sentence, I just received an email that my mortgage payment has been received.

One, I didn't make a mortgage payment. I opened the email to see what this was about and read, *"We received your recent mortgage payment of $5,000."*

Two, my mortgage is not $5,000. I logged into my account with my mortgage company and lo and behold, a mortgage payment of $5,000 had been made.

Every year in October, after I've made a year's worth of payments on time, I receive a $1,000 credit from the mortgage company. I expect this each October. Well, we must've hit a milestone year or something, because we really did just receive $5,000 paid toward our mortgage.

Boom! I'll take it!

Miraclefesting at work as I type.

Your Wish Is My Command
Lesson: Stop and notice the small things; there are miracles within

It's easy to remember the big things we've miraclefested into our lives, like Escalades, Lisa Nichols, and Tony Robbins, but our daily lives are a compilation of smaller things that we've been asking for too. The next story I'm going to share is an example of one of these moments in time and had I not written it down shortly after it happened, I wouldn't have even remembered it.

It was small and not very special. It was not long lasting and only worth a few dollars, but it was exactly what I had asked for.

I was attending a women's conference with Karen in Dallas for the second year in a row, all expenses paid, in exchange for manning a booth (yes, this was something I'd miraclefested as well). And the days were *looong*. I'm a creature of habit, and I like my morning cup of coffee and my afternoon cup of coffee. Perhaps the afternoon cup the best! As with most hotels, there was a coffee shop/gift shop in the lobby where the conference was being held, which was super convenient.

Until it closed one day by 1 pm, with many hours of the conference still left. Apparently, this was not routine practice; there was some screw up in the hotel's schedule and this was the only weekend where hours were different.

Well, that sucked, and I declared that I really needed some coffee and would find some.

I know I wasn't the only one looking for coffee and there were grumblings going on about the coffee shop being closed. The event we were attending is a class act, and being that it is, they did something about it. Not only did they set up coffee service but they very nicely and conveniently set it up in front of the booth we were manning!

There were lots and lots of booths, but it was literally two feet away from mine. As if to say, *"Vanessa, I hear you need your afternoon coffee, enjoy!"* I just had to laugh and say thank you!

And it didn't take my usual three weeks this time, maybe just an hour or so to Make It Happen. For these smaller demands, expect them to happen at warp speed and they will.

It Could Have Been Me
On The Wheatie's Box
Lesson: Clarity when asking is key

Back in my Laura Ingalls wannabe phase, I was also training to be an Olympian. Laura Ingalls by school hours and Olympic ice skater by afternoon. Every day after school, I'd grab my skates and head over to the neighbor's frozen pond to perfect my routine. Even with my only coaching being the Olympics that rolled around every four years, I wasn't too bad at the basics and thoroughly enjoyed myself.

Despite only having a few lessons here and there I dared to dream big and really thought my mostly self-taught skills may lead somewhere. Imagine who I'd be today if I'd had Youtube back then!

How I thought I'd be discovered on a frozen pond in a rural area of Colorado I'm not sure, but that didn't stop me from giving a stunning performance each day. I still love to skate and drag my family at least once a year just to be sure I can still stand up.

Several years ago, I told my husband my dream was to have a rink to myself with no one around so I could once again give the performance of a lifetime. You know, really go all out.

All out at forty-ish. It's never too late, right?

Shortly thereafter, I went to watch my nephews for a week in Northern California and we were looking for fun activities. There were no ice rinks but there was a roller rink, so we thought that might be fun.

Now, full disclosure, I also spent plenty of time on roller skates growing up and liked it well enough, but I do prefer ice skating. But hey, skating is skating and it was an activity both boys thought would be fun so we headed over during open skate time. We walked in and our "hello" echoed throughout the big empty building. We finally located someone who could at least check out a pair of skates to us and we laced up.

We were excited we beat the crowds and quickly started skating. Neither boy had skated before but the oldest one caught on rather quickly and had no problems getting off the wall and picking up speed. The younger one, under 5 at the time, wasn't really a fan and was more interested in the arcade games so he took off his skates and played games after giving it a go. That left my oldest nephew and me as the sole occupants of the rink. Not one other person showed up the entire time and we skated our hearts out until the cows came home. Literally, we had to get home and feed the cows; they live on a ranch.

As we exited the rink and began taking off our skates a lady that came in to eat lunch with the guy working asked which team I skated for? Excuse me, ha-ha, I hadn't been on roller skates in 20 + years!! But, apparently I gave quite the performance and I skated all out in a rink I had to myself! As we drove away, I remembered I had said I wanted a rink all to myself with no one watching. Well, I got the rink and no one really watching until the end. So, let me clarify with you as my witness, next time, ICE rink or pond with no one watching!

And There She Was, Right Down the Street

Lesson: Being clear on what you NEED, presents opportunities

Another of my favorite things I Made Happen drove home the point that sometimes the answers to our prayers and requests are right under our noses and we don't even realize it.

As I've already mentioned, I am in the world of retail. I'm just a lifelong peddler who loves to pick and choose what I find beautiful and pretty, well-made and unique. Over the years this has taken me down a winding path, from creating crocheted foot jewelry in high school, then interior design and cake decorating when my kids were little. I then ventured into high-end drapery fabrication sprinkled throughout the years because I love to design and sew (not clothes though!), and now, as previously mentioned I sell cute clothing.

I love to search for great products and even after all this time, I don't mind the 2:15 am wake up calls to make it to the airport for a day of buying, or the loads of packaging we do each day. I

LOVE it and it excites me! So it was no surprise when a couple or so years ago I decided I should give Amazon sales a go.

I started watching as many YouTube videos as I could find, set up my account, and began selling a few things here and there. Mostly things I personally made. Can we say labor intensive? I saw there was potential because without knowing what I was doing on Amazon, I was having a little success. But selling on Amazon is a whole different bird, and if you want to do it right, there is *soooo* much to learn.

I realized I needed a mentor; someone who was at least a few steps ahead of me and would give me a little guidance. I even wrote it down that I needed an Amazon mentor.

Fast-forward a bit—who knows, it was probably three weeks—and I was chatting with my neighbor. I told her I had been dabbling with Amazon and was trying to figure it out. She said, *"Did you know Jen (another neighbor) is selling on Amazon and she's killing it?"*

No, I didn't know that. But no surprises there! Jen is one of the most successful women I know. She's driven, passionate about business and growth, and is someone I've called on to pick her brain and ask for advice and thoughts she has about certain things.

She works a high-level corporate job; is an author, not to mention a mom and wife, and come to find out, has a thriving Amazon business. Of course, she was excelling at Amazon, that's who she is! This is a woman who does what it takes to get on the other side of the learning curve by immersing herself and studying like no other. Obviously, I really admire her and have since meeting her after moving to our neighborhood in Colorado. I immediately called her and scheduled some time to chat. My Amazon Mentor had shown up right down the street! How lucky for me.

When she realized I was serious, she literally said, "*I want to be your mentor.*" She has since shared some great insights and education with me, and I have found a successful product that makes me a little extra cash each month to put towards the kids' college. I have a lot to learn and I've barely gotten my toes wet, but there is a lot of potential and it's a profitable little side hustle.

My love for our online boutique does have my heart, but the Amazon side hustle has been worth it and I couldn't have done it without the mentor I asked for. I guess I better let her know she's in my book!

In Conclusion

Writing my portion of this book has been a huge eye-opener for me because it's really brought clarity to what my process is in bringing things, people, and adventures into my life. I've been able to identify the three-week pattern, which was not something I'd paid attention to before. I was able to discern the difference between planning for something versus it just showing up.

It excites me because it has driven me to be more firm and clear on what I want and to stand in that truth. I've got a new set of eyes on my vision board and have been able to identify why something hasn't shown up or where I've placed restrictions on it, thus rendering it dead in the water for the time being.

This has made me so ready for more; I can't wait to see what shows up next!

How could we not be excited to wake up each morning knowing

we wield that kind of power over our lives? Knowing that we have the choice to own the day, the week, the month, the year.

Life is actually much more like a game than I had realized, and playing games is fun! Just pick the one you like and put away the annoying ones. No time for that!

It is very clear to me that this is God at work; not some other supernatural power that I think a lot of us get sidetracked by. God is rewarding me for being clear in who I am and standing firm for what I believe in and what I want. Standing in my truth.

It makes sense to me that we are rewarded for trusting in him and trusting in ourselves. Making firm decisions based on listening to those nudges and whispers placed in our heart.

I love that each and every time I read through Jen's and Dana's stories, as well as my own, it literally fills me with so much excitement, love, power, and assuredness that I'm ready to run out the door to conquer the world.

My hope is that you experience these same feelings and get really clear on what you're here to win and watch the results roll in.

OMG, what can I miraclefest next?? Hint: Tahiti in June!

~ **Vanessa**

Step 2: BELIEVE

Jennifer's Stories

Introduction: Jennifer Blanchard

One of the reasons I wanted to write this book with Vanessa and Dana is because we all have totally different perspectives and experiences on manifesting the things we desire. And even though we're totally different, we're all manifesting machines.

How is this possible? Because there's no one way to manifest.

We talked briefly about the general steps in the manifestation process earlier in the book, but just to recap, the steps are:

1. **Ask**
2. **Believe**
3. **Receive**

Asking is easy. We pretty much do that step automatically. (Though not always clear enough, and that's why I'm glad to have Vanessa here to help with that one!)

Where we get caught up is Steps Two and Three.

Believing doesn't just mean creating a belief that what you want is already yours. That's part of it, of course, but the biggest factor is something not enough people talk about in a way that makes it easy to implement.

Acting "As If."

Bestselling Author and Speaker, Mike Dooley, said in *The Secret* you should spend time every day pretending that what you want is already yours, in whatever ways you can. That's what acting as if is.

Acting as if means you figure out who you'd be if you were already the person who has the thing you're asking for (see Step 1) and then you take action from that place.

For example, if you want to be a published author, you figure out who you'd be if you were already that person, and then you do the things right now that you'd do if you were already there. So as that person, you would likely have a daily writing habit; you would definitely be working on a specific book project with the intention to publish; you would have hired an editor for your manuscript, etc.

These are all things you can start doing now. And by acting as the person who already has the outcome, the outcome has to come to you (thanks Law of Attraction!).

I always say Acting As If is really just Acting In Faith of Receiving.

This is kind of a radical way of looking at manifesting, but in my personal experience (which I'm sharing in the stories that follow), Acting As If is the fastest way to go from asking for what you want to receiving what you're asking for.

Receiving is the final step in the process. The crazy part is, most of the time, this is the hardest step.

Humans have so many blocks to receiving the things they're asking for, even though we truly do want these things. I, myself, have uncovered many receiving blocks within myself over the years. (And that's why I'm so happy to have Dana here; she's a master receiver!)

And the best way I know to bust through these blocks is to act as if what you're asking for is already yours. It's how I've manifested everything from a successful business to cash out of thin air when I needed it to becoming a best-selling author in my category on Amazon, and MORE.

Acting As If is the actual secret.

My stories share how I used the principle of Acting As If to receive the things I desired. I'm sharing everything that I did and how I did it, so you can replicate it in your own life.

My manifesting skills have gotten so good I often receive things I'm asking for almost instantly. It truly feels like my life is full of everyday miracles.

But I'm not special in this way. I've just practiced a lot and been very intentional about how I show up in the world after I ask for what I want.

You deserve to have the life (and business!) of your freaking dreams. And I hope my stories will help you see how easy manifestation can actually be when you just make the decision to act your way into whatever you desire and dream of.

Dream life or bust,

~ **jennifer**

How I Manifested the Dog of My Dreams
Lesson: Sometimes you have to hold out

In early 2008, my husband and I bought our first house. We had three bedrooms, two bathrooms, a garage, a laundry room, and a yard. And having the yard made me start to think about getting a dog.

The problem was, I had always been afraid of dogs.

When I was four-years-old, I watched my two-year-old brother get mangled by a big dog. He had to go to the hospital and have stitches put into the side of his face. It gave me anxiety around dogs my whole life, including small ones.

But I'm not the kind of person who lives in fear. Plus I saw a picture of Actress, Blake Lively, holding the cutest little red Maltipoo. I told myself there was no way a dog that small could be scary.

I needed to face my fear and get a dog of my own.

All I knew was I wanted a small dog that didn't shed ('cause I hate having dog hair all over everything!). So I started researching breeds that don't shed and I came across the Toy Poodle. It looked exactly like Blake's dog, only cuter. It was exactly what I wanted.

I made a decision: I would get a red, male Toy Poodle.

I had no idea where I'd find this dog, especially considering red is one of the hardest colors to find. But I just believed and knew that this dog was already mine and that I would find him at the exact perfect time.

Along the way to manifesting my dream dog, I had put my name on a waitlist for a Toy Poodle at a pet shop near my house. One day they called me to say they had a black, male Toy Poodle available.

At this point, I had searched everywhere for the dog I wanted. I'd been emailing breeders and dog shelters and scouring the internet. It had been six months and I still hadn't found my dog.

This is when a lot of people would settle and go with the dog that's available now, instead of continuing to wait for a dog that may never be.

But I knew that if I settled I wouldn't get the dog I really wanted. And I really, really wanted a red, male Toy Poodle.

So I passed on the pet store dog and decided to hold out. I knew settling would most certainly stop me from finding my dream dog.

Another six months passed and nothing happened. But I continued to believe I would find my dog.

Then one day I received an email from a breeder I had spoken to almost a year prior. She had a litter of red Toy Poodles on the way.

I told her if one of them was a boy, I wanted him. She said she'd let me know when the dogs were born.

I knew I had found my dog. I just had this feeling my dog was in that litter, waiting to be born.

It felt done.

While on a trip to California for a friend's wedding, I got a nudge to reach out to the breeder. I sent her an email and asked if the puppies had been born yet.

She wrote back and said the dogs were born that morning— two girls and one boy.

My boy! My red, male Toy Poodle! I manifested him.

I immediately told the breeder the boy was mine, and we set a date four weeks in the future so I could come over and meet him in person.

From the moment I set eyes on that dog, I knew he was the one. My soulmate dog. The one I had dreamed about and visualized for an entire year.

Four weeks later he was ready to come home. I named him Weiland (after Stone Temple Pilots singer, Scott Weiland) and he's the little love of my life.

Sometimes when you want something, it takes longer than you think it will to receive it, and along the way, you'll be tempted to settle for less than what you actually want. But don't do it.

Hold out for what you really want. (My motto is: there is ONLY Plan A.)

Believe that you can have it. Know that it's already yours. And trust that it's on its way to you right now.

I did, and that's why I now have the dog of my dreams.

> *"The trick, is remembering that at all times far more is happening on your behalf than your physical senses will ever reveal."*
> **—Notes from the Universe by Mike Dooley**

How I Get Front-Row Parking Spots Everywhere I Go

Lesson: Make what you want your "new normal" and it will be

Last year I moved from Rochester, New York to Texas (Houston for two months, and then to Austin). Rochester is a decent-sized place, but Houston and Austin have millions of people.

Which means crowded highways, crowded stores, crowded restaurants, crowded streets. Every day. All times of day. Always.

Something I love to do is write at coffee shops (cliché, I know), and when I was going to the coffee shops in Houston and Austin, it was hard to find parking. Like, annoyingly hard.

Then one afternoon I drove to Starbucks and right as I pulled in, a front-row spot became available. I pulled in and parked. And then I had a thought, *"wouldn't it be nice if I could get front-row parking every time I went somewhere?"*

At that moment I made a decision: I'm going to get front-row parking everywhere I go.

First, I started writing it down in my journal and declaring out loud that I always get front-row parking.

Then every time I went somewhere, I would automatically drive to the front-row spots first, instead of just parking wherever was open.

When a front-row spot was available, I would park in it and then I would say out loud to the Universe, "*Of course! Thank you for the front-row parking. More please.*" These are gratitude and make-this-your-new-normal phrases I learned from my good friend, Maru Iabichela, creator of Infinite Receiving.

The more something feels normal to you, the more it will be.

And when a front-row spot wasn't available, I wouldn't make anything of it. I would just park elsewhere, all the while declaring to myself that I always get front-row parking.

Not long after I started doing this, front-row parking spots became available to me everywhere I went. Either the spot would be sitting there, waiting for me. Or someone would be pulling out as I pulled up.

This happens at even the busiest of Houston and Austin restaurants, grocery stores, coffee shops, events, everywhere. I just always seem to be in perfect timing for a front-row parking spot.

Now wherever I go—nine times out of ten—I get front-row parking. And on the tenth time, a front-row spot is about to open up, but the person is taking forever to pull out and I'm impatient so I just park elsewhere.

How I Manifested $2,500 Cash in 3 Hours

Lesson: You can have any-freaking-thing you set your mind to and take action on

It was the day before New Year's Eve 2014. I woke up in the morning to sad news: my husband's grandfather had passed during the night. We knew this meant an unplanned road trip from New York—where we lived at the time—to the funeral in Texas.

Except we were flat broke.

After he told me the news, my husband said to me, "How are we going to afford this trip when we don't have any money?" This type of question wasn't uncommon for us.

But something felt different that morning.

I had, at the time, been doing a lot of work around manifestation and using the Law of Attraction to bring my dreams to life. And one of the things that was stressed in my training was Acting As If you already have what you want.

So I had a thought: What if we just pretend we have the money for the trip?

My response to my husband was that we needed to focus on love, not fear, and that meant we had to spend the day Acting As If the Texas trip was already a done deal. So that's exactly what we did.

First, we got our suitcases out and started packing. Then I made a list of everything we'd need to do in order for us to get on the road within the next twenty-four to forty-eight hours.

Since we knew we'd be driving there, my husband took the car over to our friend's car shop to see what it would cost to do the repairs. While he did that, I got on the phone and canceled or rescheduled all of the appointments we had that week.

About an hour went by and he called to tell me the repair total: about $200. Both of us knew we didn't have the money to cover this. But since we were Acting As If, I told him to go ahead and do the repairs, even if that meant going negative in the bank account.

Within a couple hours of taking these actions, something beyond incredible happened. I can, without a single doubt in my mind, say that this was Universal magic in action.

I had a payment come in from a person I'd spoken to months before about working together, but they never pulled the trigger. And that day, the person decided to work with me.

And they paid in full.

Within a few hours of making the decision to Act As If our Texas trip was really happening, I manifested $2,500 cash—and made the trip a done deal.

Acting "As If" is a powerful manifestation tool that not enough people use.

Adults don't often spend time playing or pretending, because we're taught that those are children's games. But playing and pretending are two of the biggest ways to start manifesting the things that you want for your life.

> *"It's your degree of faith, your belief in benevolent powers, and your physical demonstrations that summon the magic...either in huge gobs or in drops and drops."*
> **—Notes from the Universe by Mike Dooley**

How I Manifested A Free Car
Lesson: Know what you want; believe you can have it;
trust that it's already done the moment you ask for it

Earlier this year, I launched a workshop called the Manifestation Experiment. The idea was to spend thirty days practicing your manifestation skills, in a safe, group environment.

The experiment was to choose one thing to focus on and manifest by the end of the thirty days.

Since I was running the workshop, I wanted to choose something kind of crazy to manifest. I really wanted to show the participants what's possible when you believe and act as if.

I'd been tossing an idea around in my head for a couple of weeks leading up to the start of the workshop: *what if I could manifest a car in the thirty days?*

The car my husband and I had at the time was falling apart more and more every day, and I knew it wouldn't last much longer. So

I decided to challenge myself. I would manifest a new car for us during my Manifestation Experiment workshop.

I was clear on it and absolutely knew it was possible. Plus, the point of the workshop was to experiment, so I had no attachment either way.

A week before the workshop began, I was driving in the junker-car with my husband, and I told him I was going to manifest us a new car during my workshop.

I believed it. I just knew that it was done. It felt done.

Because the workshop was a week out, I wasn't at all focusing on or thinking about the car yet, apart from that one conversation with my husband. I figured I'd start focusing on it once the workshop started.

Two days after that conversation—and seemingly unrelated—I got bad news from my mom: my grandpa was in the hospital and they didn't think he was going to make it. It happened so fast. He was perfectly fine one day and the next, he was gone.

It was hard to lose my grandpa. Especially since it happened almost two years to the day that my grandma died. But his passing came with a small silver-lining: my mom ended up offering me his car... for free.

It was not the way I'd have liked to manifest the car I asked for, but I know he had his reasons for leaving when he did. And I know he would be very happy that his car is now my car.

The Aerator Email

Lesson: The things you want can show up fast when
you're not attached to when, how or where you get them

One evening last summer, my husband and I walked over to
our favorite wine bar that's down the street from his parent's
house. We each ordered a flight of wine and there was even
karaoke going on. We had a blast just hanging out and watching everyone sing.

After I finished my flight, I decided to have a glass of the wine
I liked the best. It was a sweet red that was *soooo* good.

The bartender was telling me they sell bottles of that wine, in
case I wanted to take some home with me. I was intrigued, but
I rarely buy bottles of wine; I'm the only one who drinks it, and
I end up wasting most of it because you have to drink it all
within a couple days of opening it.

And then the bartender told me about aerators you use after
you open the bottle that helps preserve the wine and make it

last longer. I said out loud, "*I want one of those! Then I can buy wine more often and not waste it.*"

After finishing our wine, my husband and I walked back to his parent's house. When we were back, I decided to check my emails because I'd left my phone on the charger while we were gone.

In my inbox—I kid you not—was an email from a woman who said she loved my blog and wanted to gift me a product from her company... which sold wine bottle aerators.

And yes. I got chills.

How I Manifested A Spot In A Sold-Out 9:30 A.M. SoulCycle Class
Lesson: Make the decision and wear blinders to all other possibilities

One Friday night in 2017, my friend invited me to join her for Soul-Cycle at 9:30 a.m. the next morning. I'd been wanting to try SoulCycle out for months so I was super excited that she invited me.

The only problem was... the 9:30 a.m. class was full.

This is where most people would get stopped. But I'm not most people.

I decided right there at that moment I would be in the 9:30 a.m. class with my friend.

So I paid for a class credit on the SoulCycle app and then clicked on "join the waitlist" for the class my friend was in, letting the Universe know I planned on being there.

The message on the app said if a spot opened in the class, they'd call people from the waitlist in the order they signed up. Otherwise, the class was full and the credit would be returned back to my account.

This is as far as most people would go. They'd buy the class, put their name on the waitlist and then they'd wait.

But, again, I'm not most people.

I know that in order to manifest something you want, you have to not only be committed to the end result—getting into the class—but you have to wear blinders to all other possibilities, and you have to Act As If whatever you want is already yours. So that's exactly what I did.

Immediately after I signed up for the class, I located my gym clothes in the hamper and washed them, because I needed something to wear for the class.

Then I packed my bag for the morning because I wanted to have a change of clothes for after class, plus I packed my journal and a pen so I had something to do before the class started.

Next, I looked up where the closest parking garage to the SoulCycle studio was, so I knew exactly where to park when I arrived.

My plan was to show up 30 minutes before the class started and wait there for a spot to open. Because I fully believed that spot was already mine.

In the morning, I woke up at 7:40 a.m., threw on my gym clothes, took my dog for a walk, set up the slow-cooker for dinner, and then I grabbed the bag I packed the night before and I was off to SoulCycle to wait for my spot to open.

Just as I was pulling out of the parking space at my apartment complex to drive downtown, my phone started ringing. It was the SoulCycle studio calling to let me know a spot had opened in the 9:30 a.m. class.

Not only did I manifest my spot in the class with my friend, but since I was already up-and-about, I decided to grab a green smoothie downtown and do some journaling before class began.

Everything worked out exactly as I wanted it to because I was willing to go above and beyond what most people would do.

Most people would've been stopped by the class being full. Most people would've stayed in bed and waited for SoulCycle to call them and let them know a spot had opened.

But if I had done either of those things, I wouldn't have gotten into the class.

I Acted As If the spot was already a sure thing and did everything I would've done if it was. That's why I got into the class and got to experience SoulCycle for the first time, along with my friend who invited me to be there.

You can absolutely have, do and be anything you set your mind to. Anything!!

But you have to be willing to do the work, to take the actions and to Act In Faith that what you want is already yours.

How I Manifested Money to Buy the Perfect Blue Dress
Lesson: You must stand your ground on what you are now deciding is true for you

In February 2018, I traveled to Rochester, New York from Austin, Texas for my grandpa's funeral. While traveling, I was also running a virtual workshop called the Manifestation Experiment. The point of the workshop was to learn how to manifest by practicing for 30 days and focusing on one want or desire.

A big part of the process I was teaching in the workshop was having one specific manifestation goal, along with a pre-planned celebration that you would visualize every day as if it was already done.

I knew what my celebration was—to go to dinner with my husband at a restaurant I hadn't been to yet—but I had no idea what I'd wear. I decided that I wanted to buy a new outfit especially for that occasion.

I received an Inspired Idea to schedule a StitchFix delivery (a personal stylist company that sends you clothes to try on and buy right from home) and ask them to send me a blue dress. I scheduled the delivery for a date when I knew I'd have the money for it.

Well, the StitchFix package showed up on that date... but the money hadn't.

Without even realizing it, I fell back into an old pattern of lack and limitation. I opened the box, but I didn't try any of the clothes on. I just let the box sit on the kitchen table all weekend.

Essentially what I did was act as if I didn't have the money... and so I didn't.

The final day came where I had to either buy something or send the items back. I contemplated sending the whole box back, without trying anything on. Less temptation that way, right?

But then as I was going over to the box to put everything into the return envelope I had a thought–I need to try the clothes on anyhow. I need to act as if I had the money to spend on whatever I wanted from the box.

Even if that wasn't true at the moment.

I tried the first three items on... nah. The fits were weird and the patterns were ugly.

But then I tried on the dress they sent me. A beautiful blue dress. I knew from the moment I saw it that it was meant to be my celebration outfit.

Trying it on confirmed it.

Perfect fit. Perfect neckline. Perfect color. Matches perfectly with the shoes I had planned to wear. Looked so good on me.

I really, really wanted to keep the dress, but I didn't have the money for it.

This is where most people get stopped. They look at their bank account or their current reality that's showing them lack or limitation, decide it's true for them, and then act like it is. Exactly what I had been doing, and that was not going to manifest me the money to pay for the blue dress.

As I folded the dress back up to put it into the return envelope along with the other items, another thought hit me... *No! I don't want to send it back! I don't care if the money hasn't physically shown up yet. I know this dress is mine.*

So I took a risk. I put some skin in the game.

I decided to Act As If I already had the money and that it was just a normal month where I get a StitchFix delivery, pick out what I want, buy it and send the rest back.

I decided that I would manifest the money to pay for it in

the next twenty-four hours. I knew the Universe would support me.

I hung the dress up so I could see it first thing when I walked into my closet, and I said out loud to the Universe–

"Universe, this is my celebration dress. This is what I'm wearing. I'm buying this dress. I don't know how I'm going to pay for it, so I need you to figure it out and send it to me. Thank you."

And then I DECIDED TO TRUST.

Even though I was scared.

Even though I really had no idea where the money would come from.

Even though I was uncertain.

I made the decision that I am no longer available to not be able to afford the things I desire. And I made that clear to the Universe with my actions.

I put the rest of the stuff into the return envelope. Then I went with my husband to drop it off. On the way there, I checked my email and one of my clients had sent me her monthly payment early, which gave me more than enough money for the dress.

BOOM!!! Almost-instant manifestation!!!

This happened for a few reasons: I decided the money showing up was the only option I was available for; I put some skin-in-the-game by keeping the dress and risking not having the money show up; I stood my ground on what I am now choosing to be true for me; I delegated the How to the Universe and asked for support; and I Acted As If and took action as if I was keeping the dress—trying it on, returning the other stuff, hanging the dress up so it's a part of my closet now, etc.

This is how Acting As If equals getting the things that you desire.

But it takes skin-in-the-game actions. You have to be willing to put yourself on the line and stand your ground on what you are now deciding is true for you.

For example, if you know that the wealthy version of you would always fill her tank at the gas station—no ten dollars here, fifteen dollars there, for you—then if you're Acting As If, you would commit to always filling up your tank when you go to get gas. No matter what. No filling it sometimes and other times only putting in ten or fifteen dollars.

You have to be committed to being the version of you who is already there and who already has the things you desire to have.

I demonstrated absolute trust in myself and faith in the Universe by buying something I didn't yet have the physical cash for. And it all worked out.

When you can have that level of trust in the Universe and in yourself, you will be, do and have anything you dream of.

> *"We are limitless in virtually any way we can imagine, unless we believe otherwise."*
> **—Notes from the Universe by Mike Dooley**

The Night I Almost Got Hit By A Car
Lesson: Trust the nudges you receive

One night in my early 20s, I went to a rock concert with my husband and our friends. Because Houston traffic is so insane, we decided to park in a parking garage downtown, away from the concert, and take the train to the venue.

Soon after we arrived at the show, we discovered the parking garage we parked in closed at 10 p.m. The concert had three bands and so we knew someone had to leave early to get the car out of the garage before it closed.

Since my husband didn't care about two of the bands playing, he stayed for the first band and then went with one of our friends to retrieve the car. I stayed with another one of our friends for the rest of the show. We all decided we'd meet back up in the parking lot outside the garage later that night.

After the show, my friend and I took the train back to the

parking lot. When it arrived at our stop, we got off and then realized we had to cross the street in order to get to the parking lot where my husband and our friend were waiting.

We walked around the back of the train and were going to cross over to the lot from there. But because of where the train was parked, it was difficult to see around it to make sure no cars were coming.

We did a quick check, and then my friend took off running across the street. I followed behind him, but right before I took off, a voice in my head told me that I should skip instead of run.

Now I hadn't skipped probably since I was in elementary school. But the nudge was there so I figured, *why not?* and I acted on it. And thank God that I did.

No sooner did I start skipping, but from out of nowhere, a car came barreling down the road, going way over the speed limit. I collided with the car, smacking right into the driver's side window with my entire body. As this happened, the first thought I had was to try and push myself off the window, so the car didn't run my foot over.

I pushed myself back, just as the car braked to a complete stop. My friend had just barely made it across the street before the car arrived. And if I had been running behind him—instead of randomly getting the nudge to skip—well, I can't really say what might have happened.

I'm just grateful I didn't have to find out.

Listen to the nudges. Trust them. Take action on them.

How I Became A
Bestselling Author On Amazon
Lesson: Commit to acting on all divine downloads, soul
nudges, and inspired ideas

You know how there are dreams you have, but you don't know how they'll happen, so you don't even allow yourself to want them? That was me with being a Bestselling Author on Amazon.

I didn't believe it was possible for me, because I didn't know anyone who'd done it and I had no idea how to do it. To make that easier to handle, I just told myself I didn't care about it or want it (but that was a total lie).

And then in early 2016, I met an author who had written and published 47 books, 46 of which hit #1 in her category on Amazon. She was a bestselling author 46x over.

Seriously.

Meeting her changed my belief around what was possible, and

a thought hit me: if she can hit #1 in her category 46 times, I can do it in my category at least once!

I meant it. And that cemented my new belief that it was possible for me to be an Amazon Bestselling Author.

I made a decision: I would become a Bestselling Author on Amazon that year.

Again, I had no idea how I'd do it. I just knew that it finally felt doable.

This is a big part of manifesting the things you want; they have to feel believable and doable—and this is the most important part—FOR YOU. It doesn't help you to just believe it's possible. You can make yourself believe anything is possible.

But you also have to believe that it's possible FOR YOU.

That was something I hadn't believed before. Now that I did, I knew it was going to happen for me, even if I didn't know how or when.

Almost immediately after making the decision to become a bestselling author that year, I started receiving little nudges, downloads, and inspired ideas.

They showed up randomly; usually when I was engaged in a totally different activity. I would receive a random thought out of nowhere, and then I'd feel an inner nudge to take a particular action.

The first nudge showed up in my inbox with the subject line (and I kid you not): Become A Bestselling Author in 2016. In my mind, this was confirmation from the Universe that my ask was already done, and I just had to take action.

I opened the email and it was from one of the authors I follow online, talking about a product called Bestseller Ranking Pro, which is a software that gives you inside information about how many books you need to sell each month to hit #1 in your category on Amazon. I felt like the Universe sent this directly to me when I needed it most.

I, of course, bought the software and started to dig into the information. And I discovered something very surprising—in order to hit #1 in the Authorship category on Amazon (my category), you only had to sell about 500 books in a 30-day period (the person holding the top spot in the category was selling around that many).

Amazed that I didn't have to sell twenty-thousand books or whatever insane number I used to think was required to hit #1 in my category, this now fully cemented my belief that I could do this. I was already a published author, and I was already selling a bunch of books each month. I knew it couldn't be that hard to sell a few hundred more.

Armed with this new evidence and locked-in belief, I searched through the BRP software and found a category that had low competition (easier to rank higher in it) and lots of readers buying books. I told myself I would write a book to put into that category, and it would be an easy book to make a bestseller.

Problem is, that was me trying to mess with the hows. And the how is never up to us.

So soon after I decided I'd write a book to put into a specific category to try and manufacture Bestseller Status (hint: that rarely ever works), I received another inspired idea. I'd been running a free 30-day Align Your Writing Habits to Success challenge in my free Facebook group, and I had a thought: I should turn the content from the challenge into an eBook to help writers create better writing habits.

I became so excited about this idea, it completely pushed my plan to write a book for that specific Amazon category right out the window. I decided to first put together the writing habits book since I already had all of the content, and then I'd write the book that I'd use to hit #1 (still convinced I had to figure out the how myself).

I spent a couple of weeks putting together the Align Your Writing Habits to Success eBook, editing the challenge content, writing transitions, making sure everything flowed and linking the audio and video files. I was pumped about this book! The free challenge version had helped hundreds of writers to start building a habit around their writing, so I knew putting it out in book form would create an even bigger impact.

The week before I was going to publish Align Your Writing Habits to Success, I received another Inspired Idea: I should create a membership site where I give writers the opportunity to watch me become a Bestselling Author in 2016. And I'll show them what I'm doing along the way.

That thought scared the shit out of me, to be totally honest. So many fears and inner demons started coming up: but what if I don't make it happen? Then I'll look like a fool! Would anyone even pay for something like this? What if I fail? What then?

So I asked myself the question I always ask myself when I'm not sure what to do. I asked: what would the bestselling author version of me do? (note: you can use this as a general prompt anytime you're unsure; just insert whatever you desire to be/do in place of "bestselling author.")

Of course, the answer was, create the membership site.

As scared as I was, I decided to do it. But I still needed a name for the group.

I was on the phone with my accountability partner when a name downloaded to me: *The Bestselling Author Mastermind.*

It was bold. It made a statement. It felt really good.

I mentioned it to her and she immediately told me I had to use that name. Together we reasoned the name was aspirational and it would be my way of Acting As If I had already become a bestselling author in 2016.

I launched the group the next morning and immediately had thirty people from my community join. The energy was incredible!!

The next week, two days after the group officially started up, I published my *Align Your Writing Habits to Success* book on Amazon. The day after I published it, someone from my community emailed me to say— *"Hey! Did you know your new book is at #3 (in the Authorship category) on Amazon?"*

This was news to me! I clicked over to Amazon and there it was. My new book. At #3 in the Authorship category.

At that moment I had another download: *I wonder if I can get it to #1?*

I sprang into immediate action. I sent an email to my community, letting them know my book was at #3 and asked them to buy a copy and help me get it to #1. I posted this same message on my Facebook page and in my Facebook group. I texted friends and family a screenshot of my book at #3 and asked them to buy a copy.

Whatever inspired action came to me, I took it. For the entire day.

The next morning I woke up to find my new book, *Align Your Writing Habits to Success*, at #1 in the Authorship category on Amazon.

It happened. Three days after I launched the Bestselling Author Mastermind. And not from the how I'd come up with (writing a book to put in a specific low-competition category).

And I absolutely attribute all of this to my belief that it was possible for me and my commitment to Acting As If it was already done.

The craziest part of all, is how freaking easy it was! (I wonder how many bestselling authors can say that!)

I didn't have a marketing plan. I wasn't hustling my ass off to try and make things happen. I hadn't spent tons of money on advertising.

I just made a decision that I would become a bestselling author on Amazon in 2016, and then followed the soul nudges, took inspired action when it came to me and Acted As If it was already true.

How I Quit My Day Job to Take My Writing Business Full-Time

Lesson: Make the leap and the Universe will support you

I won't go into all the long, drawn-out history of me working a day job. The details are inconsequential, especially at this point. So let's just say, I spent seven years after college working a string of corporate jobs—that most people would consider a lifetime career—and knowing the entire time I eventually wanted to work for myself.

I began doing freelance writing in 2007 for the magazines I started my career at. This was the first time I realized I could actually make a living as a writer if I focused on it full-time.

But that didn't happen until March 2012, when I'd finally had enough of the job-jumping and doing shit I didn't care about.

I had wanted to quit my job to be a full-time writer for years. I just never did anything about it. Sure, I had a side business, but it was more like a hobby I got paid for.

All I wanted was to be able to wake up in the morning, walk into my home office and get to do work I actually cared about all day.

Thanks to Paid Time Off (PTO), Christmas and New Years, at the end of 2011, I had almost two weeks off from my office job. I had so much time off I practically forgot I even had a day job!

Until the morning of January 2, when I had to go back to the office.

It was just like any other workday. Except when I pulled into the parking garage at the building where I worked—out of nowhere—I started bawling uncontrollably. Big, fat tears were rolling down my cheeks.

I didn't want to be there. Being there didn't feel good. I couldn't do this anymore.

At that moment I made a decision: *when your job makes you cry, it's time to say goodbye.*

I got to my desk that morning, pulled out my calendar and decided I would quit my job and work for myself by May 9.

I had no idea how I'd make it happen, I just knew I couldn't keep feeling the way that I was. Something had to change. Getting yet another job wasn't going to do it.

It was time for me to make the leap that I'd avoided making for seven years.

What followed this decision was—of course—a series of inspired ideas, soul nudges and Acting As If.

I decided to clear out my desk and take home all of my personal stuff, leaving only what was owned by the company. I knew if quitting my job was a done deal that I wouldn't have anything personal at my desk.

Soon after, a blog I followed (Paid To Exist) launched an online course called Trailblazer, with a goal of helping you build a business, quit your job and get paid to be you.

It was exactly what I needed.

The price was a lot more than I had invested in myself at that point, but I felt a soul nudge that I needed to do this course. Since I didn't have the $500 up front, I signed up for a monthly payment plan, paid the first payment and asked the Universe to support me in figuring out how to pay the rest.

Funnily enough, a few days later, my mom called me and said she got a holiday Bonus at work and wanted to send me $500. I contacted the Trailblazer people and paid my balance in full.

I started doing the course and was learning and implementing. But things weren't happening as fast as I wanted them to. And things were getting worse and worse at my job.

Then one morning in March, my husband and I were

driving to work and we, as usual, got stuck in severe commuter traffic. We came to a dead-stop on the highway. We looked at each other and practically at the same time we said: *fuck this shit.*

Life's too short to be that miserable every day.

So we decided to quit our jobs right then and there. My husband dropped me off at work and he went home (he really did quit his job right then and there!) I went to the office and put in my two week's notice.

I had no idea what I was going to do for money. The future was scary and uncertain.

But I knew that as long as I had the safety net of my day job I'd never really do what it took to create a full-time business.

I had to make the leap, putting full trust in myself and in the Universe to support me. So I did.

It was the first time I made a leap that big without a clear plan and without money saved up.

Less than one week later, I got confirmation from the Universe, in the form of a letter from my 401(k) company. I never remembered receiving statements from them in the mail before, but they had mailed me a statement that let me know how much money was in my account.

Turned out I had around twelve thousand dollars saved up from my seven years in corporate jobs. With all of my job-jumping, I totally forgot I even had a 401(k)!

When I got to work the next morning, I made a call to the company and discovered I could clear out the account, all I had to do was take a twenty percent tax penalty for removing the money before I reached retirement age.

It was the best news I'd heard since I made the decision to quit my job.

I now had enough money to cover my living expenses for the rest of the year, so I didn't have to stress out about making money in my business. I could take my time getting things up to full-time speed.

I didn't even finish my two weeks at my day job. I went to the HR department on the same day I talked to the 401(k) people and told them I was out of there.

And I may or may not have danced in the parking garage as I walked to my car, on my way to living the freedom-filled life I always dreamed of.

In Conclusion

I truly believe with all of my heart and soul, and in every ounce of my being, that you can have ANYTHING you set your mind to and take action on. I live my life from this belief every single day.

That belief, combined with Acting As If, has helped me to manifest so many, many things. What I've shared here was a collection of my favorite miracles (so far!).

I hope my stories have inspired you, and shown you what's possible when you believe it is and then act like you believe it. This is the best way I know to fully embody Step 2 in the general manifestation process.

And then everyday miracles really can be your new normal.

~ **jennifer**

Step 3: RECEIVE

Dana's Stories

Introduction: Dana Rivera

What do you consider a miracle? Do you believe the only real miracles are the documented, ancient events that occurred back when Jesus walked the earth? Do you feel they are rare and inexplicable episodes, saved only for dire times and emergencies? Or are they regular happenings in your everyday life?

Your thoughts and beliefs about these sacred phenomena have a huge impact on their occurrences, or rather your recognition of their occurrences. Recognizing and receiving miracles is one of the best things we can do to tap into the energy of the divine design that is constantly giving us clues to our next best step and to our very best self.

This book is designed to help you recognize, create, claim, follow, and give thanks for the miracles that happen every single day. Through real-life examples, we can show you how Life, God, Spirit, the Universe, is always working for you and if you know how to look for it, you get just what you ask for, or better, each and every time.

I have spent the last several years tuning in to the details of my life and looking for all the ways I continue to be blessed. I have designed a full, peaceful life so that I may not only stop and smell the roses but linger, gaze, plant, harvest, arrange and enjoy the roses again and again.

I enjoy slow peaceful days at home as well as jam-packed days full of travel and adventure. I have found that just as many miracles occur with both extremes, but on slower days they are sometimes easier to recognize. When we rush through our days from one thing to another, it's much easier to miss out on all the ways the Universe is conspiring to give us exactly what we desire, or at least exactly what we put out there energetically with our thoughts.

> *"Miracles seldom occur in the lives of those who do not consider them possible. There could be a miracle waiting for you this minute. Please make room for it in your thinking."*
> **—Neale Donald Walsch**

We all have miracles in our lives and we all have the capacity to increase their occurrence. If you would like to experience even more of these sacred events, tune in to some of the subtle (and sometimes not so subtle) energies, nudges and messages, so that you too can fully experience all the magic you are given daily.

Here are just a few of the many types of miracles that have occurred in my life.

~ **Dana**

The Miracle About the Wallet
Lesson: Decide what you want and follow your inner guidance to get it

One of my more intentional miracles occurred after my husband Jay had his wallet taken from his car. (Jay is one of the best miracles in my life, but that's a whole book in itself.) The fact that his wallet was taken in the first place was just plain weird. We had just moved to one of the safest towns I have ever been to and his car was parked in our driveway, which almost never happens since we have plenty of room in the garage.

He had an early morning flight and got to his car to head to the airport and realized the window was broken and his wallet was gone. Stunned, he woke me up and I gave him his passport and the keys to my car so he could make his flight. I called to cancel his credit cards and then called the police to file a report.

Since we have almost no crime, the officer showed up in minutes. I was telling him that the wallet was the only thing missing and that in it there was a $5 bill, some credit cards that

I had already canceled, and my husband's temporary paper driver's license, which I thought was no biggie to lose since it wasn't the actual license. The policeman told me that losing the paper one is worse since a new picture could easily be photocopied onto it.

That had not even crossed my undevious mind. As soon as he said that, I became determined to find his wallet or at least his license.

The officer said there were two other cars hit that night and it seemed to be some kids or non-pros that were just looking for cash. They picked the wrong car if they wanted cash. I filed the report and scheduled the window repair and as I was hanging up, I got a knock on the front door. It was the couple next door that had found the wallet while walking their dogs.

Everything was there except the $5 and the paper license. And the bonus was that I got to meet our neighbors! Great news and my husband was relieved, but I was still not completely satisfied. The cop said it was just kids looking for money, but I did not want someone running around with that temporary license.

So, I did what I always do when I want to find something, I ask questions. In this case, *"What would it take for me to find this paper?"*

I set out on my morning walk and instead of admiring the flowers and the clouds like usual, I asked the question over and over while scanning the road near our house. I did my usual route until I got near the end of the three miles and had the urge to take a different street home.

Recognizing and following those intuitive urges is one of the manifesting steps some people ignore. Often, they don't make logical sense, or they seem silly, out of the way, or just different.

I am so glad I followed that tiny urge because I turned the corner and not very close to our house, and nowhere near where the wallet was found, I saw a small, white, water-soaked rectangle in the tall grass. Yep, you guessed it; the one thing I had hoped to find.

It was wet from the sprinklers that had been on earlier, but still folded into the wallet-size shape my hubby had fashioned.

He was so happy when I called him, and I felt so relieved that I saved him from possible identity theft and even more important, saved him from an extra trip to the DMV. He was surprised that I had found it, but then he said, of course you found it, that's what you do.

I reminded him that anyone could have found it if they asked and followed their inklings. The universe speaks to all of us, listening is the key.

> *"By thought, the thing you want is brought to you; by action you receive it."*
> **—Wallace D. Wattles**

The Grapefruit Spoon Miracle
Lesson: Ask and stay open to the possibilities

My son, Carlo and I love grapefruit. I used to serve it to him often, slicing around each section so he could easily scoop out the fruit. One morning I decided it was time to show him how to use a grapefruit spoon. Quickly he mastered that serrated edge and my mornings got easier.

With both of us using the only two grapefruit spoons we had in the house, it seemed that they were both in the dishwasher a lot, and having another one would be really handy. I realized that I had no idea where these special tools came from. Did I buy them? If so, where? Do they come individually or as a set? Do they even still make them or are they a 70s vintage item I got from my mom or grandma or thrift store?

I had no recollection of how they came into my possession. I kept asking these questions to myself with a gentle curiosity knowing that there were a few kitchen stores in town I could check with next time I was out shopping.

Two days later, I went out for my usual walk, and as I was rounding the corner to come home, I saw something shiny in the dirt under the trees on the side of the road next to our house. That looks like a spoon, I thought. *Hmmm...weird.* And also weird that I had the urge to pick it up.

When I did, I realized it was a freakin' grapefruit spoon. Right over the wall from my house. With no other houses anywhere around. I followed my urge to pick it up when I usually don't pick things up off the ground unless it is blatant garbage that needs to be disposed of.

How often do we listen to that voice from our parents or teachers that says, "*don't pick up things off the ground,*" or "*gross, that's dirty?*" Yes, they all meant well and, yes, in some cases it may be best, but it's time to use your own inner voice for guidance instead of someone else's. Only you know what is best for you in each and every moment.

So, yes, I picked it up, and yes, I brought it in the house; washed it off; put it in the dishwasher, and happily use it often.

As my good friend Oscar said when I told him the story, "*You could walk 10,000 miles and never see a grapefruit spoon.*" Thank you, Universe!!!

"There is a thinking stuff from which all things are made, and which, in its original state, permeates, penetrates, and fills the interspaces of the universe. A thought' in this substance, produces the thing that is imaged by the thought. Man can form things in his thought, and, by impressing his thought upon formless substance, can cause the thing he thinks about to be created."

—Wallace D. Wattles

The Chapstick Miracle
Lesson: Practice receiving without judging the source

My next miracle also involves a walk. I was out on a cool, windy, super dry day. I don't like wind and I don't like dry and I don't like cold, so the combination was very uncomfortable for me. But the sky was bright blue, and the spring sun was shining so it was worth it.

As I was at the furthest point in my walk, I was wishing I had put on some lip salve. My lips were uncomfortably dry and the more I licked them the worse they became. I know licking makes them worse, but the split-second temporary bit of moisture was the only thing making it bearable.

I checked my jacket pockets just in case there was some Chapstick or lip gloss or lotion or anything, but all my pockets were empty.

I was coming up on one of my favorite parts of the walk; a small lake with an arched wooden bridge. I love water and I almost always see an animal there. A crane, water turtle, fish, squirrel, or my least favorite, a snake.

On that day as I approached the lake, I looked down and right in the grass, I saw a Chapstick (with SPF 8). I took a couple steps past it and was about to keep walking when I thought, *"What am I doing? That is exactly what I was wishing for—go back!"*

So, I quickly ran back, picked it up, examined it for anything weird, took off the lid, gave it a few twists, used the lid to scrape off the top layer and joyfully slathered it on my lips.

How many of us would have walked on by, thinking it gross to pick up lip balm off the ground? Why are we so quick to judge the source of our blessings? When do we not take the gift because it comes in a way we don't expect? How many times do we pass over exactly what we want and have asked for, because it seems strange or because we don't even recognize it?

Stay open my friends, the universe ALWAYS has your back; get out of its way and let it gift you all that you desire and more.

> *"When each day is the same as the next, it's because people fail to recognize the good things that happen in their lives every day that the sun rises."*
> **—Paulo Coelho**

The Miracle Message
Lesson: Ask from a place of love, not fear

Sometimes miracles come through other people.

Years ago, I was in a very painful spot in my life. I was young and in a very dysfunctional marriage. I felt I had to get out and that divorce was the only answer. I had tried everything I could possibly think of to make things better and things just kept getting worse and worse.

At the same time, I felt horribly guilty for wanting a divorce. The bible was very clear that divorce was a sin and I did not want to intentionally do something wrong. My husband at the time, said he didn't want me to leave, but at the same time, I knew there was no way I was helping him by staying. If I was this miserable, I knew that he could not be happy either.

I met with a few pastors and Christian counselors who said there were only a few times when divorce is permitted. Abuse,

Abandonment, and Adultery are the three occurrences where God will allow divorce.

At this point in my life, I have a much different view of God and a much greater connection to my divine path, but at the time, I took this very seriously.

Yes, my husband was somewhat verbally demeaning and slightly physically rude, but nothing I could wholeheartedly call abusive. He didn't abandon me; in fact, he would hardly let me out of his sight. And as for adultery, he seemed too obsessed with me to have time for much else.

So here I was, in a position to be afraid, confused and miserable with him, or guilt-stricken on my own.

I prayed and prayed for an answer and patiently waited for some divine guidance. I would often hear a voice say, "*I call you all to peace.*" This felt like God speaking to me, but the only way I would feel peace was to get away from this guy, and I needed something more concrete to be able to move forward with a clear conscience.

My answer came... in the most miraculous way.

A friend who had moved back overseas had returned to our town for a visit. On his way, he stayed overnight in a large city a few hours away from where we lived. He decided to have a drink at a small pub near his hotel that night and ended up sitting next to a girl at the bar. As they began talking, he told her where he was going, and she told him about a fling she had a few days before with a guy from that same town.

When my friend found out the guy's name, he was floored, knowing the guy was married to me.

As he arrived into our town the next day, he happened to run into my best friend, Wendy and began asking about me. He was so confused with what to do with his new information, so he told her about it and together they decided it best to tell me.

They tracked me down and told me to sit because they had some important news they thought would be very upsetting.

As they began speaking and taking turns revealing the story, I surprised them both by leaping to my feet and dancing around the room like I just won the lottery. I did just win the lottery. I felt like I could now move on from this marriage with God's blessing and a clear conscience.

It was still difficult and painful, but I knew it was an answer to my prayers and that I was not required to stay someplace I felt I did not belong. I knew I was being called to peace and that it was better for everyone involved.

I took this miracle very seriously and I dove deep into the entire experience to absorb every lesson. I knew this was divine intervention and that all the moving parts required to get this information to me in a time long before cell phones and the internet, was nothing short of a miracle.

I have not seen or spoken to this guy since, but thirty years later, Wendy continues to be one of the biggest blessings in my life. When we can relax and have only love in our hearts and the will to do the best we can for ourselves and everyone involved, the universe always supports us.

Sometimes the best thing you can do is leave. If we are bringing out the worst in someone, let them go, that is the most loving thing you could do. God really does call us all to peace.

"A miracle is a shift in perception from fear to love."
—Marianne Williamson

My Painting Miracle
Lesson: Love things into your life

One Spring Break I was with my family at a resort in Huntington Beach. I wandered into the art gallery near the lobby and stumbled upon a painting that I fell in love with. I love many styles of art, but this was one of those paintings that spoke to me; probably because I saw the best version of myself in the painting. I stared at it for thirty minutes and asked all about it.

The curator told me what he knew about the artist and since he only used the last name, which was Schmidt, I assumed the artist was a man. I brought my husband in to see my new-found love and visited the painting every day I was there. I told my husband how much I wanted it for our house, but we both agreed that we didn't want to spend the money at that time.

I knew if I kept asking that he would have gotten it for me, so I loved the painting silently and stopped talking about it. On the last day, he offered to buy it for me, but it just didn't feel exactly right. I knew that I could love it, without having to have it.

I got the artist's business card to take with me, knowing that I was not done admiring this painting. As I walked out of the gallery, I turned the business card over and to my great surprise, the exact painting I loved was on the back of the card. I carried that card in my wallet and pulled it out to enjoy it every few days for a whole year.

The following year, my husband and I were in Palm Springs for our anniversary. I had forgotten to bring my sunglasses, so we went to the gift shop in our hotel to buy some. It was Modernism Week and there were mid-century modern displays all over town. As soon as we walked in, I felt like I recognized the artwork being hung up on the wall. I wasn't 100% sure but I was 99% sure it was the same artist of my favorite painting.

I saw a man stringing wire onto a frame behind the counter and asked if he was the artist. He said, "*No, my wife is. She will be coming in just a minute if you want to talk to her.*" As I turned around, the artist, a woman, walked in, right toward us, carrying my exact painting as if she was bringing it to me. Jay said, "*We will take that painting.*"

I broke into tears of joy as my husband and I began to tell her the whole story. I showed her the business card in my wallet and told her how I often admired the image on the back. She was so taken with my love for the painting that she gave us a generous discount, signed the back and took a picture with us.

Her sweet gentle spirit and her appreciation of my love of her work was magical. The painting is one of my treasures and still hangs prominently in our home today (and it is also on the cover of this book).

When we think we need to hurry and take things for our own, we are coming from fear. When we can appreciate something and not have to own it, that's when it becomes ours, that's when our vibration is a match for it.

Admiration and love are what brings things to us. Fear only drives them away. Just like with people, when you can love them and respect them without having to own or control them; real love blossoms.

> *"Not what we have but what we enjoy, constitutes our abundance."*
> **—Jean Antoine Petit-Senn**

The India Trip

Lesson: Keep your desires alive and stay open to receiving them

I have been wanting to go to India for several years. The only person who knew my great desire was my husband. He has been to India once before we met and has absolutely zero desire to go back.

I would often wonder how I would visit India. Since most of my big trips are done with my husband and sometimes other couples, it didn't seem like anything that would likely happen, at least not soon. But I continued to wonder and silently ask how I was going to get there.

One day this past spring, I was on a plane headed home and I got a text from one of my best friends, Denise, asking if I wanted to go to India with her. "*Well yes, of course I do!*" I replied. She told me it was a girl's trip that another one of our friends had planned and sent me the itinerary.

I literally welled up with tears of joy as I read the different destinations and experiences. It was exactly what I wanted to see and do. And the price was very reasonable.

I wasn't sure how I was going to pay for the tour and the flight, but I was more than sure I was meant to go, so as soon as I got home, I went to the website to sign up. I found the website and the tour date and as I filled out my info and hit the button to sign up, the page flashed "THIS TOUR IS FULL." *Noooooo!* I was too late. It was all booked up.

I took a deep breath and trusted that what was happening was for the best.

The next day I called Denise to tell her that I had tried to sign up, but was too late and how sad I was that I wasn't going to be able to join her. She told me she had already given them my name and they were holding my spot. I was so elated and back to the original excitement.

When I told my husband that I had signed up to go on a Girls trip to India, he was not only happy that I got to go, but even more thrilled he didn't have to.

A few weeks later, I began looking for flights. I knew I wanted to upgrade my seat so I could sleep in a bed and start my trip rested and refreshed. I had some air miles, but nothing seemed to be working out well with times and dates. I would be flying from a different city that the rest of the group and I didn't want to arrive to India by myself.

I have learned that buying flights when you are frustrated or uneasy, is not the best idea. That is something best done when you are feeling light, calm and happy. So, I stepped away from the computer, knowing that I would have better luck another time.

My birthday was a couple weeks later, and Denise called and told me she had a gift idea for me but wanted to make sure that I wanted it before she bought it. It turned out to be the most perfect gift in the whole world—a business class flight to India. Not only do I get to sleep and feel pampered the whole flight, but I get to travel with my sweet friend the whole way.

Wow! Talk about a beautiful miracle!!! And a loving, generous friend.

> *"And, when you want something, all the universe conspires in helping you to achieve it."*
> **—Paulo Coelho**

Mulch Can Be Miraculous Too
Lesson: We are angels for each other

One spring day a couple of years ago, Jay and I went to Home Depot to buy new flowers for our front yard. We ended up needing way more than we realized, and the weather got a lot hotter by the time we got home.

It would take us hours to plant all these beautiful new flowers and we really wanted to get it done before the rain came that night. Because my hubby and I aren't afraid of a little manual labor, we dove in head first and started digging and planting.

We decided we needed new mulch for the yard as well, and that we also needed some help planting if we were going to get this done before the rain started and before we had to get ready for a party we were going to that evening.

Just a few seconds later, a guy drove up in a truck with a giant pile of mulch in the back (the exact kind and color I like) and asked if we needed help. Not only did he work alongside us planting so much faster than we could, but he finished it off with the beautiful mulch as he brought joy to our garden and our day.

I know that he was our angel and, yes, I also know that we were his. He got to sell his mulch, his time and his muscles AND he got to hear me call him an angel at least seventeen times.

We were his angels and he was ours. Talk about a win-win.

"All God's angels come to us disguised."
—James Russell Lowell

The Surprise Income Miracle

Lesson: We don't need to know the 'how'

We have some property in a little town in northern California. It is commercial land with no buildings on it. I had written down on a manifestation exercise that I wanted to receive income from all our properties. I didn't even think of this property since so far it has only been property tax bills for the last fourteen years and I never saw a way we could make money from it unless we built something on it or we sold it.

The next month, we got a letter from CalTrans that they would be doing some road work and wanted to know if they could rent the property for two years to store their equipment. *Well, yes you may, thank you very much!*

I had no idea that was even an option. You just never know what surprises can pop up when you throw it out into the universe without any doubts attached. Most of us ask for something and then think about all the reasons why it can't work, it won't work or that we don't deserve it.

There is an infinite number of possibilities for how things can work. Sometimes we can't even see one of the ways with our limited minds.

It is easy to see and believe what is physically in front of you. It is much harder to trust in the non-physical or formless happenings that are in constant motion around us.

God has plans so much greater than anything our narrow and sometimes fearful minds can come up with, so when we can relax, trust and stay open and curious, answers and events unfold in the most miraculous ways.

> "To think according to appearance is easy; to think truth regardless of appearances is laborious and requires the expenditure of more power than any other work man is called upon to perform."
> **—Wallace D. Wattles**

Housekeeper at the Door
Lesson: We attract what we think about with love and curiosity

My nephew came to live with us for a semester. We were very excited, and I thought with an additional teenager in the house that I may want some extra help with the cleaning and laundry. I do have a lady that comes regularly to do the big cleaning but wanted to make sure we were organized on a daily basis.

Most people would start researching and asking friends, but I chose to do what I normally do, and just wonder and silently ask where I'm going to find some help.

That very same afternoon I got a knock on my front door. That rarely happens, so unless I'm expecting someone, I usually ignore it. This day, I decided to answer the door, even though I was on the phone at the same time. (Doubly unusual.)

When I opened the door, to my delight, it was Maria, our cleaning lady from three years ago who had moved to Mexico to take care of her father. She was back in the states and looking for work.

It turned out after a couple calls back and forth that she found a full-time job and I could easily manage the cleaning and laundry on my own. But just the fact that she came knocking on the same day I was wondering about a housekeeper is a miracle that I adore!!!

> *"Miracles are a retelling in small letters of the very same story which is written across the whole world in letters too large for some of us to see."*
> **—C. S. Lewis**

Car Accident Angels

Lesson: Angels are always with us

When I was in high school, three friends and I got in a car accident. We were driving back from the beach at about 2 am on a narrow, twisty canyon road. There may have been wine coolers involved.

I was in the passenger seat and I am not sure what happened, but the car went straight when the road turned to the right. We flipped upside down into a ditch and landed with the hood on a boulder leaving enough room, so the roof of the car was dented but not crushed. Once we realized we were all OK, we managed to get out and climb back up onto the tiny canyon road.

As if on cue, a giant sedan came driving by with two old ladies in it. They stopped and offered us a ride home.

There are so many miracles in this story; it's amazing.

First, no one is usually on this road in the middle of the night, especially two old ladies in a car big enough to hold six people.

Second, we were all barefoot and none of us cut up our hands or feet climbing back up to the road. The next morning, my dad wanted to see what had happened, so we drove the twenty minutes to the site of the accident. When we saw all the broken glass, sharp rocks, and steep slope, I was shocked that we could have all climbed up so quickly and even more shocked that we weren't shredded up.

Next, the fact that we crashed off the left side of the road is the reason we are alive. The right side of the road is a steep canyon that is hundreds of feet down.

Another miracle is the boulder we landed on. If that wasn't there to provide a small pocket for the roof of the car, we would have all been smashed.

The tow truck driver couldn't believe I was in the car the night before. When he saw the totaled car, he said he thought for sure that any passengers were dead.

The two ladies who picked us up told us they were coming back from a conference. Really? A conference at 2 am, from Malibu? I say they were angels who came to show us four kids that divine intervention is constant and that we are always surrounded by God's loving presence.

"The more gratefully we fix our minds on the Supreme when good things come to us, the more good things we will receive, and the more rapidly they will come; and the reason simply is that the mental attitude of gratitude draws the mind into closer touch with the source from which the blessings come."

—Wallace D. Wattles

Muscle Testing Angel
Lesson: Our growth and expansion are always supported

My family and I moved to Texas in 2013. We didn't know many people, and I was happy to live anonymously for a little while. I took this alone time to go on walks and dive into my spiritual learnings and personal growth even more.

There was one technique I was particularly interested in learning about and that was muscle testing. I had done a little here and there but wanted to learn everything I could about it. I read a few books but realized I wanted an in-person class where I could physically see and experience it.

I didn't even know where I would find a class like that but just wondered. So, like I do, I went on a walk. During my walks, I would listen to Hay House Radio on my phone. I knew the schedule pretty well and had my faves.

This day, I walked a little later than normal and Dr. Fab's show was on. Dr. Fabrizio Mancini is a health and wealth coach with a long list of credentials and I knew of him, but I had never listened to his radio show. I knew Wendy was a fan, so I was excited to hear him. When he said his special guest for the day was LaRue Eppler, the queen of muscle testing, I was glued.

I listened to her sweet voice and heard talk about Texas. I thought, *oh wow, I wonder if she is coming to Texas?* Then I heard her say Dallas (which is near where I live). When she gave her website, I ran home with chills.

I looked at her site and found out that she was doing a seminar fifteen minutes from my house three days later for $35. I signed right up and sent her an email saying that she and her class is just what I had been wanting. She emailed right back saying that she felt a connection with me too and couldn't wait to meet me.

LaRue has become such an amazing part of my life. Not only is she a dear friend, but she has helped in my growth, my family's growth, my friends' growth and I even worked for her for over a year.

She and I are having lunch on Monday and I can't wait to tell her she is in my book. She is one of the best examples of an Earth Angel I know; she is a blessing to each and every person who knows her.

In addition to having LaRue in my life, she also introduced me to Dr. Fab. He, too, has become a great friend and has blessed my life in so many ways.

When you can stay open and curious, the answers always come. And often in better ways than we can even imagine.

> *"The value of consistent prayer is not that He will hear us, but that we will hear Him."*
> **—William McGill**

Island-Hopping
Lesson: Love it into your reality

Back in 2004, my husband, Jay, and I took a sailing trip with some friends around the British Virgin Islands. It was one of my most favorite vacations ever.

Years later, in the cold, early months of 2016, I told Jay that I really wanted to do a trip like that again. We talked about how amazing it was and agreed we would love another island-y voyage.

After looking into the price, we realized we had some other things to spend money on that were more pressing than a luxury sailing trip. But I continued to send him pictures of the catamarans and beautiful blue water on a regular basis and assured him that somehow, we would be going on a trip like this soon.

Later that same year, Oscar, one of our very best friends, started planning his fiftieth birthday. Oscar knows how to celebrate, and part of the festivities included inviting some of his friends on a catamaran in the British Virgin Islands. We were blessed to be included in that small group, and not only that, but he and his wife Denise were treating us on the biggest catamaran I have ever seen.

Needless to say, we had the time of our lives and I am forever grateful to have been included in that, and the many celebrations that my friends and I enjoy.

Never did I worry or think about the "how" we were going to get to the BVIs or the cost or the reasons why we couldn't go. I just enjoyed the pictures and shared them with my husband as I thought about the beauty and the fun and the feelings I have while there.

The joy brings the gifts; the fear keeps them away.

> *"Whatever you hold in your mind on a consistent basis is exactly what you will experience in your life."*
> **—Tony Robbins**

Hurricanes Need Love Too

Lesson: Our focused love is more powerful than we realize

While we were on that magical trip in the Caribbean, we got news that a hurricane was coming in from Africa. We had a couple of days before it would hit, but the captain and crew began preparations, which included reserving rooms in port and finding the safest place for the boat.

We continued to have fun while the crew constantly watched the weather updates. That evening while we were at a restaurant on shore, I said to our friend, Kenny (who has a giant amount of love and energy), *"What we resist persists. We are going to love this storm back into the ocean to be dissipated. Are you ready to help me?"*

Since we had done some energy work together in the past, he was more than ready! This was Oscar's birthday trip, and nothing was going to keep us from enjoying it to the fullest.

As soon as we ran out to the dance floor and began to do our "Love the Hurricane Dance," the Toto song, "Africa," came on. (and this was a year before the popular Weezer remake) Seriously, of all the songs to come on; we were clearly in the vortex.

Since Kenny is a little younger than I am, he didn't know the words. When I began to sing along in my horrible, loud voice, "*I bless the rains down in Africa*," he knew the universe was listening and that we had the power to love and bless this storm into tranquility.

We woke up the next morning to news that the storm had shifted and all danger was gone. Not sure we could have dissipated Hurricane Irma, which hit the following month, but I am also not sure that we couldn't have.

Focused intention and love are some of the most powerful things in the Universe.

> "*The basic stuff of the universe, at its core, is looking like a kind of pure energy that is malleable to human intention and expectation in a way that defies our old mechanistic model of the universe—as though our expectation itself causes our energy to flow out into the world and affect other energy systems.*"
> **—James Redfield**

My Clothing Business Blessing
Lesson: Follow your desires AND your gut

Just before my son Carlo started preschool, I knew I was ready to do a little work. I didn't want a full-time job or anything stressful, but I wanted something creative and inspiring.

Several years before, when I was a single mom to my daughter, I thought about opening a clothing store. I had found the perfect spot in downtown Napa; an empty storefront that used to be a dress shop. But for anyone who knows Napa, downtown was not always the happening, fun place it is now.

It was a rundown town of either outdated or empty stores with very little foot traffic and very little tourism. I saw the potential and I saw the opportunity, but I also saw the risk, and I wasn't willing to take that as a single mom with no one else to rely on.

So, I kept my desire but followed my gut and got a job in the accounting department of the biggest wine company in the world. I am very grateful I did since I loved my job, learned a lot and met some inspiring people.

Now it was six years later, and I was a happily married stay-at-home mom; my husband had a great job, and I had time and energy for something I was passionate about. After talking with Vanessa (the co-author of this book and one of my closest friends), we realized that she had the same type of dream way back when.

We heard about a few companies looking for reps to host home clothing parties. Not only did we not like the clothes or the prices, but we also didn't want to work for anyone else. We wanted it to be ours and we wanted to do it our way.

So, we created our own business model; taking only the bits we liked from other companies and coming up with our own. We had a boutique right in my house and we called it *Blush*. Our kids could be there; shoppers could bring their own children and babies; we set our own hours; served coffee, wine, snacks, and See's candy; and only worked when we wanted.

Vanessa and I both had big, beautiful pearl-white SUVs (one of her great manifestations), so we could take our boutique on the road and bring the clothes to new people. Our following grew and so did our fun.

That company, *Blush*, was a blessing for me for eleven years. It gave me a friendship with Vanessa; we laughed and had the best time almost daily. It gave me connection, since we got to know hundreds of women in our town and many more friends of friends in other towns and other states. It nourished my creativity and my love of accounting, business, and learning. Then when Vanessa moved to Colorado three years in and I was sad to lose her daily company, it gave me the confidence that I could do it alone and still be successful.

We continued our monthly buying trips to Los Angeles together, which really helped with the separation anxiety. Then in 2013, when my family and I moved to Texas, *Blush* allowed me to go back to Napa every month to do my trunk shows and to see my girlfriends and goddaughters. And when the Napa fires hit and I felt helpless being so far away, *Blush* helped me feel useful when I was able to donate all the clothing to those who had lost everything.

It has been a year since I donated everything and dissolved the company, yet *Blush* still brings me joy since Vanessa and her daughter have carried it on in Colorado. I still get most of my clothing from them (www.blushoutwest.com). Go shop, you will love it!

My early dream of having a clothing business became so much more than the store I once imagined. The love, miracles, friendships, and money that came with it, never once brought stress or family sacrifices that many business owners experience.

When you have a dream, be open to altering it so it works for you. If you don't see a job you like, create your own job, company or career. The ideas and miracles are endless.

"Do not go where the path may lead, go instead where there is no path and leave a trail."

—Ralph Waldo Emerson

The Man and the Dog
Lesson: There are no coincidences

Here is another story that involves Vanessa and probably one of the wildest stories I know.

About ten years ago, my two kids and I were visiting Vanessa and her family in Colorado. At the time, my daughter really wanted a dog. She and Vanessa's daughter were both eleven-years-old and obsessed with dogs.

Vanessa's family had just gotten a dog and my kids wanted one too, especially my daughter. Now, my husband and I are not big animal people, but we had adopted a dog several years before and it did not work out well. This dog was very energetic and shed everywhere.

We didn't have the lifestyle, the yard or the patience for her. After she badly scratched our friend's son in the face while trying to play, we knew it was time to find our little doggy a new home. I hear all you animal people getting upset with us, but I guarantee you that we found the perfect home for her. She was treasured and loved, and we got to visit her regularly. She couldn't have been happier, and neither could her new owner, who had just lost his longtime canine bestie and just happened to be a ringleader for dog shows.

After that episode, the thought of a hyper, barking dog, was enough to disturb my peace. And the thought of fur, poop, and pee was enough to destroy my husband's super clean, tidy ways. So, we knew getting another dog was not for us.

My daughter continued asking, and on this visit together with Vanessa's daughter, they took an online quiz to find our perfect dog. Turned out our family match was a Schnoodle. Well, back in 2009, I had never heard of a Schnoodle.

"What in the heck is that?" I asked.

They went on to tell us that is was a Schnauzer and a Poodle mix and showed pics of how cute they were. I had to say, they were very cute. So as our days in Colorado went on, all I heard about were Schnoodles.

From Vanessa's house, my kids and I went on to spend a few days with my brother, Clay, and sister-in-law, Jill, in Vail. After our visit there, they took us to Denver to have lunch and do some shopping.

My daughter asked if we could go to a pet store. I assured her that if we happened to see a pet store in downtown Denver, that we could definitely stop in, knowing darn well that we wouldn't see one. Not one minute later, we come upon an SPCA storefront, right on the 16th street mall.

My girl was so excited and asked if we could go in. I said *yes*, as I am not one to easily go back on my word. So, the two of us went in while Carlo walked on with Clay and Jill.

She climbed into the window display with a bunch of puppies and I found an armchair where I could relax. A dog jumped up on the chair with me and just snuggled right into my lap. As I sat there petting the dog, I was thinking about how this dog actually made me feel even calmer.

I was so used to dogs stressing me out that I was a bit surprised. As I was thinking this, a man in a suit walked into the store. He asked if I was getting a dog. I told him, no, but my daughter really wants one.

He and I ended up talking for over a half hour and I was so taken by him. He spoke with such wisdom and love and told me all the reasons I should get a dog. He told me how his wife is deaf, and they have a hearing dog for her. It picks up on sixteen different sounds, such as the telephone, doorbell, timers and buzzers and also sirens and horns while she is driving.

I asked him what kind of dog it was, and he told me it was a Schnoodle. Well isn't that just a coinkidink? I told him that was the type of dog my daughter wants and how I have always loved the look of Schnauzers but didn't know much about them. He told me all about the breed and all the benefits. He also told me about his daughter and his job and how his office was upstairs, but his big projects were in Boulder, which is about thirty miles north of Denver.

Whenever his job got stressful, he said he would come down and pet the animals and it always made him feel grounded and peaceful.

I seriously could have talked with him for hours. I wanted him to be my dad (even though I have a great dad already), or my uncle or my neighbor or something. I just couldn't get enough of this man's loving wisdom.

Finally, it was time to leave. My daughter had found several dogs she would have loved to take home. At the time we lived in California, so there was no way we were getting a dog in Colorado. Clay, Jill, and Carlo came back to get us, and I tried to explain the conversation I had just had but realized that I couldn't do it justice without sounding like a weirdo, so I finally just dropped it.

I called my husband and told him that I think we need to get a dog. His exact words were, "Fuck no!" which made me laugh because, of course, we didn't need a dog, but after my time with the man, and my new dog friend, I was convinced that we did.

Clay and Jill drove us back to Vanessa's house which is about forty-five minutes south of Denver. As soon as the girls were back together, they were Googling Schnoodles again.

I began telling Vanessa all about my experience with the dog and the conversation with this man. Being the dog lover that she is and seeing how I was suddenly open to getting a dog, she was very intrigued.

My kids and I were flying home the next afternoon, so Vanessa and I got up early to do a couple of our favorite things; have coffee and go on a walk. As we walked, I continued to talk about the man and the dog and the entire experience. Vanessa said she wasn't sure what a Schnauzer looked like and as I was trying to describe it a lady came by walking a Schnauzer.

We were in awe! We walked a few minutes more and we saw another Schnauzer sitting on someone's porch. We were not walking through a regular neighborhood, we were walking through large open spaces where each house was on at least an acre or two.

Vanessa does that walk regularly and not only had she never seen those dogs but she rarely even saw a person. She looked at me and said, I think you need to get a dog! I agreed with her; it was far too powerful of messages coming at me.

When we got back to her house, we packed up our things to head to the airport. On the way, I asked Vanessa to stop some-where so I could get my kids some food before the airport. She knew of a deli that was good, but I said a Starbucks might be better for my picky kids.

She said she had seen one up the road before but had never been to that location. She found it and we all jumped out of the car. It was about 11:30 am., so it wasn't very busy when we walked in.

I noticed one guy on his laptop in the back of the small shop. He was wearing shorts, and a t-shirt and his energy seemed familiar. We all ordered and as we were waiting for the food, the girls found a table and were back to Googling Schnoodles.

The man seemed so much like the man from the day before, but I knew that was impossible. There are well over three million people in the Denver metro area, and not only that, we were so far from Denver and even double far from Boulder. But I couldn't help thinking it was him.

His drastic change in clothing and the lighting made it really hard to tell. So, I yelled Schnoodle to the girls to see what he would do. Well, he looked right up, and our eyes met. I almost fell over. Like almost fainted. I had to hold on to the counter while I said, "*that's him*" and Vanessa, as shocked as I, said, "*She has been talking about you all morning.*"

He seemed like he was almost waiting for us and was not shocked or surprised at all. I told the girls about his dog and he asked if we had a few minutes. He called his wife and had her come down, so we could all meet his wife and the hearing Schnoodle.

Needless to say, we got a dog. She is a rescue dog, so we don't know her exact breed, but she is part Schnauzer, part Poodle and who knows what else. She doesn't shed, rarely barks (unless it's the UPS truck or the pool guy), and she is the calmest most peaceful dog I know. Almost ten years later, we are all still over the moon about her; even my husband.

> *"There are no mistakes, no coincidences. All events are blessings given to us to learn from."*
> **—Elisabeth Kubler-Ross**

A Miracle Since Writing This Book
Lesson: You attract what you energetically broadcast

As you can see, miracles come every day. Several miracles have occurred for us since writing this book. If we kept adding them, we would never go to publication. So, this is my last one.

You read about my painting story and meeting the artist. Well, in choosing a cover design for this book, the three of us agreed to give a few ideas each and go from there.

I got the idea to see if we could use the painting that I so love on the book cover. I wasn't sure if this was even possible, no idea if it would cost thousands, no idea if my book mates would like the idea and no idea if I could contact the artist. So, I followed my desire and stayed open and curious.

I searched for the artist and found her website and her phone number online. I left a message with my questions and ideas and in case it was a cell phone, I also texted her the photo of her and me with the painting to see if she would remember me. She called right back and we had a long conversation; she remembered me and was thrilled with the idea. She told me that it was perfect timing for her and that she had her own miraclefesting around that exact painting, which happened to be her very first gallery painting.

I asked her if she would like to write a piece for the book and she was very happy to do so. Not only does she do energy healing and life coaching like I do, but she is a cancer survivor and does an array of practices to help raise the vibration of the planet. She has also written several books and my call has inspired her to publish them.

No wonder I was so drawn to her painting and so drawn to call her. We are an energetic match and are now phone friends. I look forward to learning from her and her deep loving wisdom.

In an email to me she wrote:

> *"It is amazing how synchronized the Universe is when we flow with its ever-perfect timing! Nothing happens by accident! We seem to connect on more than one level in our frequencies. Now is certainly the time for manifesting the good works you've been percolating with for some time. I am very happy for you and look forward to your book! I wish you the very best of success and I am so happy you reached out to me."*
> —**Tina Schmidt**

Here is Tina's story about the painting:

Miraclefesting Miracle

Tina Schmidt's Story

When I was a kid, I wanted to be an artist. So, I continued to hone my skills and eventually hoped that one day, I would make my dream come true of having my work in galleries. I loved midcentury modernism and I loved the old movies from the 50s and 60s.

My life journey took me to many different jobs and experiences, but I kept holding on to the dream of being a gallery artist because it meant that someone felt my work was worthy of being recognized.

As I began to crystallize my vision, I drew a pencil sketch of the painting on the cover of this book, "Miraclefesting." I carried that small pencil sketch with me for over a year before I actually started painting it. I kept looking at it, envisioning what I wanted to do with it, how I would develop it, and what it symbolically meant to me.

I frequently looked at the sketch and kept building a meaning and purpose with it. Eventually, the time came for me to bring it to life! At a time in my life when I had some serious physical challenges, I decided to move forward with the painting because I wanted to keep as much positive vision for my future as possible.

While painting it, it came alive with all the energy and love I had bottled up inside me for so long. I threw my heart and soul into it! It was the Rosetta stone and the beginning and first expressed passion of my vision and my desire to be a gallery artist.

When I made the work public, I was immediately picked up by a Palm Springs Gallery! The painting was a hit and sold at the art show! Later, I was picked up by several other galleries and thus began my professional art career as a gallery artist!

My vision I had held onto, the sketch I started with, the painting I finished with, and all the dreams I had associated with it—all came together in the most magical of ways!

I've made hundreds of paintings since then and have enjoyed selling originals and prints alike, reaching out to people and sharing my work with them. It's a dream come true!

Now I deal direct with the public and make not only mid-century modern works, but sci-fi, fantasy, and abstracts as my love and vision continues to expand and reflect a variety of creative endeavors. The artwork has become a means of reaching out and touching people's lives and making them happy.

As a cancer survivor, I realize that the most important thing about my creative work is the positive energy and joy it brings to people. If we can bring more love, harmony, and joy to people during our life, we are leaving people with the greater Good that extends beyond ourselves. And this, for me, is motivation enough to keep me going!

So, I say to people, "Keep your vision of the future! Keep your desires alive! Life will take you to where you are supposed to be and bring all the gifts you never expected at the right time and right place if you never lose your vision for what you want.

*~ **Tina Schmidt***

In Conclusion

This is just a tiny sampling of the big and small miracles that have been a blessing in my life. As you can see, miracles come in all shapes, sizes, and circumstances.

I urge you to look at your own life and see where you have been a part of the divine picture. Where have you received a miracle and where have you been the miracle for someone else?

Also, look at where you have blocked a miracle or gift by judging it, feeling like you don't deserve it, feeling like it's too easy, too hard, too weird, or it's just not what you expected. Even refusing or dismissing a compliment can block the flow.

For any blessings to come, there needs to be a clear energy field; aka no resistance. That means, no doubt, no fear, no conflicting messages about your desire. If you say *"I want it but..."* you are keeping it away. Once you realize we are all deserving of anything and everything we desire, the resistance fades and you get to choose.

The Universe is like a loving parent. We all want our children to have what they desire. We just need to know what it is they want and why. Once we know, we want to do everything we can to help them get it.

So speak up, ask, then listen and follow the nudges and know that you have the ability to get what you desire, or something even better. As we become even more connected to the Oneness and release all doubts and fears, we can't help but experience our thoughts and desires.

Here's to You and Miraclefesting!!

~ **Dana**

About the Authors

Jennifer Blanchard

Jennifer Blanchard is a multi-passionate author, screenwriter, storyteller, developmental book editor, writing mentor, coach, t-shirt collection owner... and whatever else she feels like being and doing. She stands against choosing just one thing; believes you can be, do and have anything you set your mind to and take action on; and is a living proof example of it.

Jennifer helps multi-passionate writers, creatives and visionaries live their purpose and do their soulwork. She currently resides in Austin, Texas.

Vanessa LeVan

Vanessa LeVan loves flowers, fabrics, and finds beauty in the details of pretty things. Give her a beach, a book, a sewing machine, and coffee and she's one happy lady. She was born at the beach, raised in the mountains and started her family in a valley, lucky to have lived in the places vacations are taken. Vanessa is a creator, boutique owner and enjoys supporting other women in their life and business, letting them know they are not alone.

She now resides in Colorado with her husband and is some-times an empty nester with two kids coming and going. They have a dog that sheds all over and a cat that glares at them.

Dana Rivera

Dana Rivera is a writer, teacher, student, life coach, and a lover of life, especially the spiritual world. She was born and raised in Los Angeles and jokingly credits that with her ability to receive messages from the angels and from divine wisdom.

She loves to travel and see new things and has moved 39 times (that she remembers). She embraces change and growth and does her best to be a better version of herself each day. She practices a variety of techniques to clear old patterns, beliefs, and fears and is passionate about helping others do the same. She loves to see how small shifts can bring great joy.

Although this is her first book, she has been writing stories, songs, and poems for years. She knows with more love, we can all have the joyful, meaningful and miraculous lives we came here to experience.

Dana has two magnificent children, a wise, loving, fun husband, the best girlfriends in the world, and a cute dog named Daisy.

MORE FROM THE AUTHORS

Jennifer Blanchard

Jennifer offers developmental editing services and workshops for multi-passionate writers, creatives and visionaries; hangs out on:
Facebook (facebook.com/dreamlifeorbust);
Instagram (@JenniferBlanchardWrites);
YouTube (youtube.com/jenniferblanchard);
and blogs over at www.dreamlifeorbust.com
and www.jenniferblanchard.net.

Vanessa LeVan

You can find Vanessa and her online boutique at:
www.blushoutwest.com,
www.facebook.com/BlushOutWest/
or IG @Blushoutwest.

Blush Out West ~ styles rooted in the west, helping you feel feminine and confident.

Please join our Facebook Community: www.facebook.com/ miraclefesting and follow our Instagram www.instagram.com/ miraclefesting to share your everyday miracles big and small with us. The more we recognize and give thanks for them, the more we will all receive.

Dana Rivera

Dana does virtual energy healing sessions and loves to help people make easy shifts to find even more joy and peace in their lives. Her website is: www.danarivera.com

www.miraclefesting.com

About the Cover Artist

Tina Schmidt began her career in 1979 with her first sales in sculpture. She cultivated her skills as a 2D and 3D artist through the 80's and 90's, working as a sculpture and illustrator for the Gaming Industry and Entertainment Industry. She created model designs and limited edition products for the Disney Store's Princess series.

Tina worked for well-known companies such as Lorimar Studios, Warner Brothers, Disney, Clasky Csupo, and Nickelodeon. As a Supervisor and Animation artist (background development), she worked on shows like "Rocket Power," "Rug Rats," and Ronald McDonald Direct-to-Video production shows. She also taught animal drawing (including animal behavior, anatomy, and biomechanics) and perspective drawing (layout and design development) for 16 years at Cal State University Fullerton. She retired in 2015 but continues to pursue her interests in creative endeavours.

Aside from these professional jobs and experience, Tina continued to expand her interests in the mid-century modern era. As a child from that era, she appreciated the history and culture that emerged from the Atomic Era where dreams and visions of the future caught the whole world's attention.

Tina Schmidt's Mid Century Planet art is a salute to the iconic pop culture of the past revitalized by today's modern collectors. Her "Retro-Fusion" paintings are a fusion of lifestyle, fashion, design, interiors, and iconic architecture of the 1950s, 1960s, and includes sci-fi lore. Her paintings go well beyond the surface of character and settings to that of whole environments where shape, light, form, and shadow play an important role in the visual storytelling.

Swanky lounge glamour, chic women, men of class and high expectations, social gatherings, poolside martinis, and even rockets, spaceships, and aliens of the Atomic Era--all come to life as the signature elements of her paintings!

34069313R00104